WORDS TO BE PERFORMED FROM UNDER A TABLE BY THE LAST OF US

James S M Parker

This collection of poetry, sketches, short stories and observations sits between (inside and outside of) 'Love or Suicide and the Life In-between' 'this heat, it's hell closing in on me' and 'broken will always be broken'.

'Words' looks at the writer and his relationship with words and their meaning in his life, a life now completely unravelled.

'To be performed from under a table' looks at the observer existing in a hole he cannot escape, full of despair and rage.

'The last of us' looks at the suicidal mind as it travels through its own hell, dead but very much alive.

They each interweave and compliment not only each other but the three other books mentioned in the first paragraph. Indeed, it will be possible to read all four of my books in an order as to complete the jigsaw piece presented within my work; within myself.

James S M Parker 22/03/17.

Cover design inspired by Mark Cassell – see back cover insert

The Author asserts the moral right
to be identified as the author of this work.

ISBN 978-191117-569-8

Printed and bound in Great Britain.

Published by YouCaxton Publications

WORDS

WORDS

WORDS

WORDS

WORDS

WORDS

WORDS

WORDS

WORDS

WORDS

WORDS

WORDS

WORDS

WORDS

WORDS

WORDS

WORDS

WORD s

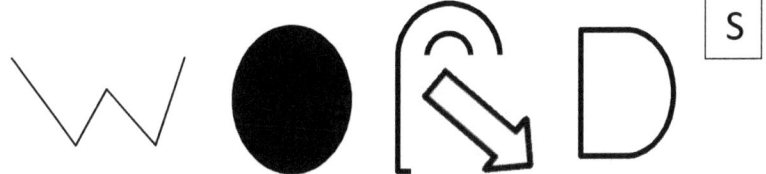

to be performed from under a table

BY

THE LAST

OF US

This is…

Visions of new worlds created by black ink
Characters from within, landscapes from without
Existence both living and dead, truth and lies
Thrust upon the reader, a game about to begin
Twisted and wrapped around the Author's fingers
Moulded into clay and puppets, the sadist
And placed upon a clean blank page
Amongst a land of punctuation and inserts
Surrounded by the scattered ash of "the rule book"
Its home? A graveyard of other so called guides
Full of scavengers and used as playthings
Their un-original insides out on show for all to see
Jealous of the true dreamers over the horizons
The bones of inspiration alive and breathing
A timeless portrait of the lone writer
With only a frail shadow for company
Burning with ideas and new possibilities
This compass keyboard shining with red water
A whiff of heat and deceased prints
Beaten with absolute meaning and passion
Raw emotions dance across poetry and prose
The antidote to the poisons of conveyor life
A slaughter of the 9-5 monthly wage depression
We seed made up lands with heroes and villains
Deep and serious, shrivelled yet strong, black and white
Open wounds demand an uncompromising stare
Bodies sold and used, broken and begging, ripped
Stitched together with stone and button skin
Conflicts raging through these scripted tears
Whilst single letters and numbers are granted souls
An overdose of options, fonts and styles damn and save
Leading to the light at the end of the tunnel
Our own demented ideal of the reader
A reflection of who we are and what we have experienced
Good or bad, lost or found this is…this is…
The day words came to stay.

a writer sits alone on a leather chair in front of a desk. a writer is surrounded by inspiration and project planners. a writer has one lamp, one hot drinks coaster, one mouse mat, one ruler. a writer has the cd system close enough to plug in headphones. a writer has an abundance of pencils that will never get used. a writer has a sharpener just in case though. a writer always has multiple projects on the go. a writer only ever drinks coffee. a writer has far too many coffee mugs. a writer drinks way too much coffee. a writer sits a bit too close to the laptop. a writer needs to know the time at all times. a writer suffers from numb bum all too often. a writer has a varied and very interesting bookcase. a writer sometimes uses a glue stick. a writer sometimes uses tak. a writer sometimes uses a nail and hammer. a writer has the desk next to the window. a writer looks to the stars. a writer is a dreamer. a writer looks around a dark room when thinking. a writer taps on the keyboard when deciding. a writer rarely smiles. a writer eats when writing. a writer fidgets about constantly. a writer has tired eyes. a writer has a brain that never sleeps. a writer writes better to music. a writer has a back that clicks and cracks. a writer has more than one calendar. a writer believes to be the best. a writer will think the worst. a writer has on average of 689 ideas per day. a writer remembers on average 2 ideas per day. a writer doesn't feel the cold. a writer does feel the heat. a writer in the zone is an entity possessed and driven. a writer thinks outside the box. a writer is not afraid. a writer keeps lists of lists. a writer can get distracted by something so very small. a writer explores entire universes. a writer feels the tapping of the keys through his fingers to his twinkle toes. a writer writes shit. a writer has some disgusting habits (nose picking and farting especially). a writer hates punctuation and spelling. a writer has a favourite type of pen. a writer hates the 9-5 job. a writer uses the laptop as a piano. a writer is jealous of song lyrics. a writer always has a pile of dirty washing that needs cleaning. a writer stares into the light for a bit too long. a writer has that one distinct word that is used in everything written. a writer is always writing. a writer is never truly alone in this world. a writer can never decide between 'normal' and 'no spacing'. a writer finds peace in games. a writer doesn't believe in the word or actions of 'no'. a writer likes to help other writers. a writer has a lot to write about. a writer appears in every single thing written. a writer wears comedy slippers. a writer will write even through illness. a writer will own a marker pen but rarely use it. a writer likes the smell of cork. a writer has a shadow that writes. a writer has a very sweet tooth. a writer wishes to be a musician. a writer walks on a tightrope. a writer can wait forever for an idea. a writer really likes the word count display at the bottom of the screen (666). a writer is never finished. a writer formally hates the television (but deep down inside loves it). a writer views the world as if it were an unfinished novel. a writer is a writer for life. a writer is a writer in death.

But what do they mean?

In reality, what do those words mean?
How do we digest their meaning?
How do we know if we understand them?

I wish you would die.

What does that mean?
Does it mean an enemy wants you to die because of hate or a beloved one wants you to die because you are suffering with some form of pain?

All words mean something completely different to every single one of us.

Poetry.
A book.
Lyrics to a song.
An article in a magazine.
The headline in a newspaper.
Instructions for a flat pack bookcase.
The review of a film we desperately want to see.

Words shape our very existence, make us who we are and build on our very being; past, present and future.

But what do they mean?

You tell me!

It's an information overload

Words tell me what it is
words tell me what is in it
words give me advice
words say 'yes' and 'no'
words mean I can sing along
words paint a thousand pictures
words tell me where I am
words tell me what to buy
words show me a way out
words give me bad news
words congratulate my achievements
words instruct my task
words tell me who to thank
words line up my bookshelf
words feed me when I am hungry
words can get me drugs
words help me learn new things
words can give a rousing speech
words can make you laugh
words guide the blind
words give hearing to the deaf
words keep you to a deadline
words can free your mind

and

words hide an information overload

even though

words can be eaten
and sometimes shouldn't be said

apparently

words cannot describe our love.

Paralyze me with your words

Paralyze me with your words,
make my mind go completely numb
and shock my body into a frozen state.

Paralyze me with your words,
hurt my feelings with past desires
and shatter me with your cold touch.

Paralyze me with your words,
line up verses with a haunted delusion
and twist the poisoned knife deeper in.

Paralyze me with your words,
burn away my tainted flesh
and embrace the screeching of my pain.

Paralyze me with your words,
as I weep for release from this truth
and pray for a swift death.

The Light

I can see it, just there,
a light that shines brightly,
its gaze showers me,
its longing draws me nearer,
beckons me over with a smile,
waves at me with a familiarity…

…it's a sunrise,
it's a full moon,
it's life,
it's death,
it's me,
it's you,
it's ghost…

…this path…this light.

And the softly spoken words twinkle with a motion of the stars,
its sheer will pulls us ever nearer to this final exit,
taking us away from a life lived and lost in a memory,
taken from a sadness with the realisation of so much more…

…oh this light.
This brilliant light.
How I love thee.
Your embrace.
Your whisper.
Your future.

The light,
it will shine for everyone.
The words,
they will speak to everyone…

…this path…this light…these words.

The Smell.

How do they smell? Oats and raisins packed with sugar cane?
Smouldering ash drifting through a summer morning – hearts and keys?
Bring the smell to me...I want to gorge on it and twist it round my little finger!
It's home cooking. It's comfort food.
It can be whatever you see it as.
Iron blood on a stone plateau.
Bleached worktops glistening against paper light.
Fear pouring from an open wound caused by the shock of the new or the loss of the old.
Bring it to me...these words surround my senses.
Make me smell myself. Make me smell my own being. Make me smell my reactions.
Reactions to what my eyes are reading.
Reactions to how fast my heart is beating.
Reactions to how my soul is feeling...oh such sweet words.
How do you do the things you do to me?
How can your aroma fill me with dread and joy? Anger and love. Pain and relief.
I never just read the words
I experience the words.
I smell the words.

The Smell.

hcfywgudipqoksjkwfhjgreuyhuivrjpigkrnjkbruguyreg
hvuioijkejhbfugweuyhdiuwpodkomjcnherbfueguyerhgv
uihsjcnjerhreuygciuewhoijcxkewnjfbrefyughuiejjwh
sgwvrsdresdxdsxhfvdhnkgjoiihioyjjhntubygcyhbhcjn
oeniorthygryuwguyebjiwnjxmedkgvxgwvtdtywtyuiwdoi
wiofouewfyewghjhewhgwevxghvgyfctywergcuyhwrfuher
ufjreiuhjfuckuiwhfywebfuicweuhdiuhiuxuygwtqfyrws
ftywxgvchbcuienvonournvbuortnvojnoncoienvcuiubci
ubgeyugcuyergvuihoiajvhivujbiuberivbhourevouewno
icvneoujenoenroicnoeroifnveoloadsoijourehuvbreib
viewbicycbewiycbiewbciubwiucbuirebufuywftdczytwv
uxyhuiscbuioeniobjnirtnbuienruovneouvnoincoienoi
vofoiwjciowneoucbiwyevcyvcyivuibadshyrrqwdsfcfvh
jcjknvnmroivjeruhvyiwgvihwbcjhwbjwbiuebiujhcuhwe
tvctyuervcyubrecniuwuiyueuwtoireyoeriuiwhijewbyu
twuiowqpqpfjjwvebhewordsuwnchbewhcbewuvcwyuevcyu
ewcibwejcnwejfnuiregurhiubiucbocwoicxniowencuiby
wcgtywtycqtycgvxhbwijcniortobirhbuiwbviueuibuicn
iwonvioheourghuwhouwbcuobcuowbuocbwoutoiuqhygwey
cvyuwbcuiqwbuocnowvnuoewvuhweuvhguiwbvubwejvnjew
vbuiewgywgeivghwoiviowncionwoueviuvguergubhihvwe
ihvoiwq0uvbwoibiobivbniwbvenipowbiobiowbiefindiw
jevoiwevoiwiovnwoievnoiqwvoiqhvuohquqyutqfxvqhxb
kwvjoirogpeogjwioryqegvchwckjewogjejghvuoewvbouw
evnionqnionwoevbwouvuowhgoiqefnioqwncnqwuchuoweh
ogwehoignwvhuiecanoiuwhvuwhvouwouv0oiewncioewnoi
voiwhregouyruwgoiwjgipowjoivnowkienciponwipoevno
ineboeroihbyouuochqucbiwebcjiwebjovwebviywtygyou
ergoieroibjnjknjhbshquzagvhahcjisoislajkahdyiegr
fvyebiuvbeivouenoenoinbonoeroibnwoinbvoibnouwebo
uewouvbownoiegnbowuegbowheobnwoinvoiwnhcbwibvwui
bvouwbouvbnownvobwouevbouwbvouewfindthemalloqnco
iwnvoiwnvouwervuobwouvnbwocnoiqncioqnwcionwouvnb
ouewrbvouoinwiobnipwnvpinqpiencpoiqncpiqnwpivnpi
eiqpieguiuytiewyuiwejgioqwocnowmotherfuckeroiqjc
iowenvouwebhbuvewiubvouwcbnoiqwncoinbwiubvbviweb
vguiwehiuhqwvjoiwnvojbweobvoiwrebviowboh

don't you just love a word search of complete nonsense?!? or is it complete nonsense?!?!?!?!?!?!

How you gonna see me now?

How you gonna see me now?
With words and plastic plates.
Block letters and a forced bow.
Furrowed brow, heart that hates.

How you gonna see me now?
With keys and blinking lights.
Inmates ride an enormous cow.
Concepts reach imaginary heights.

How you gonna see me now?
With debit cards maxed out.
Nothing to show for it...wow.
Head high this mystery snout.

How you gonna see me now?
With full stops ending your words.
Punctuation revolving their rows.
Flying crosses mating with birds.

How you gonna see me now?
I'm nothing more than a blank page.
You will never see me now.
Locked in this computer cage.

We're all crazy.
We're all crazy.
We're all crazy.
We're all crazy.
We're all crazy.
We're all crazy.

I can fly

And with these words I can fly…

…soaring over peppermint skies,
skirting on an odyssey of clouds
and drifting towards our brilliant sun…

…and with these words I can fly…

…a mesh of emotions heightened,
dancing with my heart on a string
and swirling this infinite love…

…and with these words I can fly…

…inspiration feeds my minds freedom,
allowing creativity to fill a blank page
and gives a voice to my ghost…

…and with these words I can fly…

…I graze and prosper thanks to you,
I open my eyes to look at you,
I have two ears to listen to you,
I turn my head to pay attention to you,
I feel just to hold you,

and with these words I can fly
and never let you go.

<u>Define me</u>...please

(because we all need definition to feel comfortable and safe)

"the smallest unit of language that can be used independently; such a unit represented in writing or printing."

a small unit of language
put together to create
a large
a meaning
a desire

something so small
becomes so big
a crazy diamond
forever immortal
part of infinity

tiny letters
portrayed with size
told with passion
felt in heat
tears in rain

holding a book
smelling its soul
tasting its print
watching it breath
living in its world

a small unit of language?
most definitely not!
a beginning
an end
a life.

depression

I went to the Doctor today,
was told I suffer from depression...
...his words, not mine.

I can't contain it anymore,
can't hide it from prying eyes,
can't deal with it without help.

Drained from exposing myself,
drained from having to open up,
drained from having to accept.

Now, I have to pop some pills,
read a booklet and look at a website,
report back in 4 weeks...on time.

How can I tell them it won't work?
How can I tell them I have no future?
How can I tell them it is inevitable?

I am so tired of life.
I am so fed up of just existing.
I am so tired of wishing I was dead.

how can you tell someone that the love you had for them has gone?
the intimacy you once shared is no longer there.
the flame has been replaced by a smouldering burnt out wick.
that special spark damp to the core.

what words can you use to do this?
in what situation is it going to end well for all parties involved?
pretending is just as bad as lying.
and living a lie is not living at all.

there is an empty void in the pit of your stomach.
and you hate yourself for letting this happen.
but still remains a sliver of doubt about "the right thing to do".
this question still hangs over your head.

maybe this is just a phase, something you will get over with time.
a midlife crisis born from other aspects of your life?
a build-up of pressures caused by just simply living.
maybe...maybe not.

and in the end, a distance has crept its way between you.
bodies together but souls stepping apart.
and deep down, both of you know what has to be done.
no looking back...no regrets.

but that isn't true.
this will be a regret.
this will be "that moment".
broken heart.
lost mind.
<u>dead soul.</u>

search for some sort of meaning,
I grasp for some sort of reality.
The screams drown out my heartbeat,
the hate inside turning me cold.

Empty blood from fresh cuts,
an empty soul from fresh scars,
every scar telling a different story
each with the same ending.

<u>It's sad really.</u>

I was telling myself today...

...that it wouldn't be so bad if I killed myself.
I wouldn't be missed for that long,
wouldn't be mourned much.

I mean, everyone has to deal with their own problems,
everyone has shit going on in their lives,
what do they care about someone who isn't there anymore?

Words cannot describe how I am feeling,
I can't articulate the thoughts rushing through my mind
or express the deep void consuming my being.

I am no longer living anyway,
merely existing stuck on repeat,
who wants to live like that?

I was walking past a parked up lorry,
thought about laying underneath it
and having it crush the life out of me.

Struggling to get up and out of bed,
struggling to get through the working day,
struggling to enjoy the weekends.

I was telling myself today,
using suicidal words and thoughts,
that it wouldn't be so bad if I killed myself.

Suicide (part 1)...

...is a state of mind where words cannot help.

Powerless to ease the suffering in the mind,
helpless to heal the wounds on the body.

Take away the S and the U and the I,
mix the letters around a bit and what is left?

Dice. Suicide is a roll of the dice.
You can roll a 1 and feel ok.
You can role a 3 and feel so lost.
Or, you can role a 6 and mark yourself...keep score.

So tell me, what words help with that?
What phrase full of punctuation and capital letters can ease that sort of pain?

Suicide is a state of mind where words cannot help...

Suicide (part 2)...

...is a state of mind where words cannot help.

At first you take little nicks,
nothing more than a tiny scratch.
Enough to see skin turn pink,
enough to feel a slight sensation.

The next time you draw blood,
nothing more than a few drops.
Enough to see skin scar up,
enough to feel some discomfort.

Finally you cut across a vein,
nothing more can be done to stop it.
Enough to see the crimson flow,
enough to feel your life empty on the floor.

Suicide is a state of mind where words cannot help...

Oh Death...

...what words do you have to comfort me?
What words will accompany us across the river?

Was my life full of meaning and worth?
Will I be remembered with a wry smile?
Did my time count for something?
Please, oh Death, what was my legacy?

Did my actions help just one person?
Was I supportive enough to those who needed it?
I listened to the talkers, didn't I?
I cared for the lost, didn't I?

Oh Death...

...what words of advice do you have to guide me?
What words will accompany us into Hades domain?

Am I to be herded off with the sinners?
Or welcomed with open arms by the saints?
Do I have a special slot in purgatory?
Please, oh Death, what is my place?

Does it matter how or why I died?
Isn't the sacrifice I made enough punishment?
I won the unwinnable, didn't I?
I paid for the poor, didn't I?

Oh Death...

...what words of strength do you have to help me?
What words will accompany us whilst in this Hell?

Does my sentence match my crime?
Am I now a part of this gallery of suicide?
It was my decision was it not?
Please, oh Death, what is my suffering?

Will I wear these scars even in Death?
Are they a warning to those who pay a fleeting visit?
I cut sacred flesh, didn't I?
I ended my life, didn't I?

Oh Death...

...what words of torment do you leave me with?
What words will accompany me for eternity?

gravestone

How could you sum up you in a sentence?
What message about you would you leave for all to see?
Carved in stone, etched in time forever,
till the end of all things.

Are there words you could use?
Is there a message you want to pass on,
a message of truth, advice, humour…death.

For our gravestone is our end.
Our gravestone is how we will be remembered.
Our gravestone is our final words.

Tears

Bring me sunshine, bring me tears,
bring me a burning light, bring me fears.
So few answer, so many questions,
now a lack of colour, scratching blackens.

Shed tears of anger, and of hate,
brought on by an act of check and then mate.
A mess of words confused with meaning,
a legacy left behind full of seething.

Dried up wrists lay loose upon a stained bed,
a gleaming white carpet now soaked blood-red.
Lifeless eyes stare into a separate realm,
a locked grin frozen; the point of overwhelm.

Deep down, they now know he is free,
his release unlocked by the suicide key.
Despite the sorrow he leaves behind,
this was his act to himself of kind.

Words of Wisdom

Stay away from the pornography
Your bank is not your friend
Just breathe
The gym is not your friend
Put the kettle on
Life is not your friend
Be yourself
Arrogance is not your friend
You only get one chance in this world (depending on your beliefs)
Addiction is not your friend
Don't drink and drive
Television is not your friend
Be careful how and when you pat a cat
Your neighbour is not your friend
Glue is not there to be sniffed
Old age is not your friend
Screaming your balls off can be very good
Golf is not your friend
Masturbation is not evil
Time is not your friend
What goes around really does come around
Money is not your friend
Fruit and Veg are good for you
Alcohol is not your friend
Don't piss off a gorilla
Routine is not your friend
Comedy is not meant to be taken seriously
Work is not your friend
Sex is very good for you
The sun is not your friend
Learning is also very good for you
Technology is not your friend
The world is not flat
A sharp object is not your friend
Respect gains respect
Dust is not your friend
Giving to charity is a good thing
Anger is not your friend

Smile every so often to passing strangers
Buy one get one free is not your friend
A healthy body leads to a healthy mind
The "man" is not your friend
Experiment with your body and mind
Substance abuse is not your friend
Love or Suicide and the Life In-between is a great book (as is 'this heat, it's hell closing in on me')

A symphony

Plucking, dancing, creeping notes sway in shadow corridors,
these pieces of music haunt and tug away on captured fears,
an almost impossible task to use words to merit a symphony,
an almost impossible task to fill a blank page with sound...almost.

Thick strings accompany a lone guitar passage,
building layers of pure feeling and tangible angst,
piano keys explode with blinding fury
giving way to heart beating drums that crash and crunch,
this storm corrosion reaches for the heavens,
threatening to destroy all in its path...until,
until a frail single voice gives birth to words,
oh such sweet words.

And with these words come misty meaning,
a sodden tour of stories and experiences
of a person's travels against the life living,
slave to the barriers of politicians and the fellow man,
an accompaniment of pain and salvation,
hand in hand with love and suicide...until,
until it builds to a silent crescendo and explodes,
a symphonic tear.

This bombastic sound drowns out such sweet words,
igniting a passion once upon a time thought lost,
bringing with it a raw sticky heat,
invading the pores on your skin
and violating dormant silicon brains,
these past masters bring with them power...until,
until serenity beckons us over and smiles
the dawn of silence.

Dangerous, beautiful, inspired notes sway in shadow corridors,
these pieces of music breathe and feed away on captured fears,
an almost impossible task to use words to merit a symphony,
an almost impossible task to fill a blank page with sound...almost.

It's in the lyrics

Feel the music,
dance to the beat,
but never forget,
to listen to the words.

Lyrics tell a story,
describe an emotion,
feed the instruments
and give life to death.

They bring meaning
and connect with us.
They describe reality
and soar with fantasy.

Heartfelt, never cold,
lyrics grab hold
and never let go,
become part of our portrait.

And it is then that we realise,
then that we understand,
that they are so much more than words,
more a symphonic collection of poetry.

Granted there are many soothing and warm words – there are also cold words. Harsh, bitter, cold.

NO…NO…NO…NO – the

coldest of

them all!!!!!!

Hate, hurt, death, revenge,

scourge, kill…………

TO HEAR THESE

WORDS

TO FEEL THEIR EFFECTS

TO SPEAK THEM AND

THINK THEM

IS COLD…SO COLD.

they poison

they cut deep

they rip apart

they sicken

a cannibal corpse of letters and punctuation...

AND SO WITH YOUR HELP, WE CAN RID THIS WORLD OF THESE HORRIBLE AND COLD WORDS. WITH YOUR HELP WE CAN GIVE TRUE MEANING AND POWER TO THE WARM WORDS, THE FLUFFY WORDS THAT CAN MAKE US SING AND DANCE AND LAUGH AND SKIP ABOUT IN LOVELY GREEN FIELDS WHILE BIG SPONGY WHITE CLOUDS DRIFT OVER OUR HEADS THAT SHINE IN THE MORNING SUN...SWEET. SO SO SO SO SO SO SO SO SO SO SO SO SO SO SO SO SO SO SO SO SO SWEET.

Sorry…

…for your loss

…to hear that

…for shouting

…I didn't mean to hurt you

…for eating all the biscuits (right now, I am currently eating chocolate crunch creams)

…I missed "whatever"

…in advance

…for being a dick

…for getting it wrong

…I don't remember

…I don't love you anymore

…for giving away the end

…for leaving the toilet seat up

…I wasn't there for you

…I didn't quite get that

…did you fucking say something

…is that too loud

…who are you again

…sorry sorry sorry

Our Soldiers

In muddied boots and damp helmets,
trudging across a land of mines and graves,
they fight for a reason lost in translation
and die for an excuse in education.

At home, politics and banks blind our senses,
dazzle us into a naïve arrogance,
what is happening to our sons and daughters?
what is happening to our human race?

They cling on to humanity through family,
they cling on to life through each other,
they cling on to reason through orders,
they cling on to hope through a future.

And still the bullets and mortar rarely miss,
the guns and ammo rarely run out,
the madness and sanity rarely differ,
and the beginning and end rarely change.

But they still go on,
and we still send them in,
and they continue to fall,
and we continue to fail...

...to stop the fighting,
stop the suffering,
and stop the loss.

Tears of a Generation

Watching baby soldiers from the glazed rear window,
in the old peoples home surrounded by post war survivors,
I drift back to my time dug in trenches and surrounded by minefields,
remembering orders to sit tight,
remembering orders to dig in,
remembering orders to fight on.

The dawn would come and go and the dark gave way to frost,
friends fade, diminish and walk off in the distance of a dream,
their actions and heroics all summed up in a letter signed and stamped,
remembering mothers and lost sons,
remembering wives and lost husbands,
remembering sons and lost fathers.

My generation fought with the world against an obvious evil,
our actions shaping and defining this life taken for granted,
those left behind a reminder of mistakes and lessons not learned,
remembering crosses and remains,
remembering medals and doves,
remembering poppies and graves.

And now baby soldiers pass my glazed rear window,
off to fight this lens tainted war of stained terror and black oil,
in lands of sand and sun, surrounded by bombs strapped to man and machine,
remembering home and humanity,
remembering cause and effect,
remembering reasons and honour.

Our sons and daughters, grandchildren and friends,
should be moving forward, not being dragged back,
the world wars of a generation a warning to those who didn't listen,
remembering death and pain,
remembering loss and sorrow,
remembering tears of a generation.

untitled (how original)

sorry is the hardest word to say
an admission of wrong doing
an admission of guilt

words of wisdom, words of hate, words of love
display off
and a picture that can paint a thousand

we plan, we buy time
but do we say what we really mean?
or mean what we really say?

I saw God
in a cracked mirror
on a broken ship

man overboard
drowning in nouns and verbs
for our entertainment

who are you? who are they?
in five words or less – describe yourself -----------------

it's alright to lie…

…because

love is the hardest word to feel
an admission of being in
an admission of falling

the road we take
the words we use to get us there
the words we use to keep us there

page up, page down
and home is where we end up
our own little odyssey

a floating paw
a wink and a smile
a snapshot in time

we freaks of nature, capable of beautiful speak
yet we lock ourselves away
in a clockwork cursor - |

<u>Save me with your words</u>

Tell me you love me
Tell me you need me
Tell me you care for me

Tell me I am important
Tell me I will be missed
Tell me I mean something
Tell me I am not just a number
Tell me I am part of this world

Tell me this is just a phase
Tell me this will all blow over
Tell me this will get easier
Tell me this is not the end

Tell me we will be forever
Tell me we are as one
Tell me we are special

Save me with your words
Save me with your words
Save me with your words
Save me with your words
Save me with your words
Save me with your words
Save me with your words
Save me with your words
Save me with your words
Save me with your words
Save me with your words
Save me with your words
Save me with your words
Save me with your words
Save me with your words
Save me with your words
Save me with your words

...because only your words can save me.

words on a keyboard

look at you keyboard, what words can you make just by glancing at the letters for 1 minute:

hub
kill
saw
fred
drew
look
pool
pill
jump
jug
thunder
sax
chump
hurt
raw
tree
point
hung
crew

AaBbCcDdEeF

fGgHhIiJjKkLl

MmNnOoPpQ

qRrSsTtUuVv

WwXxYyZz

Now – imagine what you could do with all those letters????

Imagine the words you could create using them????

Imagine the worlds they would inhabit????

...And so to you, humble reader, from me, your humble narrator...what are some of your favourite words? Please use the box below to indulge yourselves:

PERSONALLY, I HAVE ALWAYS LIKED THE WORD ~~'FANNY'~~. IT CAN MEAN SO MANY DIFFERENT THINGS TO SO MANY DIFFERENT PEOPLE!!

Why will these words not help?

Over and over they taunt me.

Revel in my pain and hurt.

Drink in my misery...

Sick fucks!!!!!

End.

"I need to get away from these words and hide. I need to get away from this life and disappear. I need to climb underneath that table!"

when comfort runs dragged across bare arms in
lines of red and scratchy scratch

and darkness is the colour of coffee that swirls
around sticking to white teeth

an attempt to sew shut the voices using thrash
stitching and death needles

keep you locked in coffin of slinky coldness
dripping with a brilliant hatred of me

your arms tired from pushing the ones to the edge
of ceramic forgiveness

all the while protecting and comforting the he
inside of the me

this fighting an odyssey of celluloid reverse
promises grinning with lies

guiding your carcass over trenches of worn out
scars and fresh skin

and what's left but a frightened shell shivering
under a table of wood

a splintered performance with a bow to the
crowd and a pitiful applause

to be performed from under a table...

there are always four walls
there is always a ceiling
there is always a door...
...and there is always a table.

there are always two people
there is always a third
...there is always a lock
and there is always a table...

there are always creatures in the night
there is always a bogeyman
there is always a mirror...
...and there is always a table.

Headmaster: Yes hello, do come in
(the man walks in and sits down in front of the Headmaster who is sat behind his desk)
Man: You wanted to see me?
(the man says crossing his arms)
Headmaster: Yes I did
(the Headmaster replies eyeing the man up and down)
Man: Is this about my son Johnny?
(the man says clearly agitated)
Headmaster: No, not exactly
(the Headmaster shuffles in his seat)
Man: Then what?
(the man snaps throwing his arms up in the air)
Headmaster: Well, it's about you
(the Headmaster opens a file on his desk)
Headmaster: Don't you think it's time you...well...moved on?
(the Headmaster says cautiously?
Man: What do you mean, move on?
(the man leans forward in his chair)
Man: What does that file say...
(the man points at the file...and then at himself)
Man: about me?
(the man leans back in his chair)
Headmaster: Well, it says you have been with us, in this school as a student for quite a long time now...
(the Headmaster pauses for a long time)
Headmaster: and surely it must be time for you to, you know, move on
(the Headmaster closes the file)
Man: Move on? Move on! But I'm only 40...
(the man says)

Calorie burn in California

people often say to me ‘ why do you ride round on that?’

‘ride round on what’ I will say back with a sarcastic tone and with one eye closed

‘on that’ they say, sometimes getting angrier, sometimes just sounding confused

‘on what’ I would reply, my voice taking on a California twang

‘on that exercise bike’ waving their arms in the air like a deflated balloon puppet man…or woman

‘well’ I would start

‘you see’ I would continue

‘I don’t like gyms…but I love exercise bikes so’ I would almost finish

‘I thought to myself why not stick a couple of rubber wheels with spokes in on an exercise

bike…look, I have even attached some brakes that can be operated on the handles’ I would

demonstrate

‘but’ would always come the reply

‘why not just go out and get a proper bike?’ their eyes swirling in their sockets

‘because’ I say very slowly because I hate repeating myself

‘I…don’t…like…gyms’ and then I would ride off

Sing it out loud...with your ear pressed to stinky carpet

Your vision reduced to square reflection glass,
free ear listens to dust mites scutter and blink,
as the clouds boomerang concrete overhead pass,
and your piss fucking IQ heads downwards sink.

Toe nail tap on back of radiator al you min I um,
distracted by handheld bitter batter splatter,
an altar of photo fake worship to those some,
characters available to use just grave fatter.

These faces stare blank cold and pixelate,
a chambers dictionary of babble twit and twat,
the need in constant pride stretching update,
bringing with it a techno pool of jam crap.

And when body lay bloated dead in real life,
unfollowed by thumbs up weep melancholy,
chose to forgot you flowered with wife,
your chemical marriage nothing but folley.

I was walking down the street one day carrying a book and some bloke came up to me and asked me what I was carrying. I said it's a book. He said what's one of those then. I said you know, pages with words in...a book. He said he'd never heard of one, said I was being mental. I said what do you mean you never heard of a book, you must know what one is. He swore he'd never heard of a book and asked why I was carrying a square. A square I said, it's not a fucking square, it's a book. They must be rare them things he said cuz I never heard of them. Fuck off I said, you must have heard of a book, read them in school or at home. We never had them in our school he said, you must have gone to a posh one. Of course I didn't go to a posh fucking school I said, books are available in most schools. He said they weren't available in his school. What school did you go to I said. The London Grange he said. Fuck me I said, that's the most expensive poshest school in the UK, how the fuck did they not have books. Well they didn't he said. So you never read a story I said. Of course I've read a fucking story he said, just not from one of those books. What I said. I read stuff on my phone, got one of those Apps he said. What the fuck is that I said. An App for your phone he said, means you can read stuff on the go and carry it in your pocket, You are fucking having a laugh I said, and you're calling me mental. Look, I'll show you he said and he pulled out this small oblong fucking shiny thing. What the holy fuck is that I said. It's a phone he said. A phone I said...what the fuck is a phone.

Inevitable

Colour fading reflected through silent photographs
Framed in space, locked by memory still
A stark comparison to this place of ending
Dying light casting shadows over the caught
Captured frailty and years eclipsing our two lovers
Bringing them a knocking, welcomed, celebrated
For their quality of life outdid them all
Sharing every moment, weathering every front
A joining through all levels, all doubts
Strength beyond weakness, tears finality
Past, present and a future epilogue over
As their thoughts lock and reason the 'what is'
Accepting of the inevitable, the fact
Of the blindness to come, the warmth to cool
Save for their very last breath to utter promises
And bring about their journey and peace
It was time to blow the candles out.

Imagine silence...

Imagine a world on mute, its heart beat silenced.
Imagine the excitement of children
and their choir of fun and youth hushed,
their voice taken away, their energy sapped.

Imagine watching images, colours driving by.
Imagine seeing a change in her
and the emotions it will bring,
her feelings of love and hate quiet, her life subdued.

Imagine reading lyrics, words that need sound.
Imagine smelling the smoke
and not hearing the fire burn,
its relentless consumption, its deadly lick.

Imagine studying time, hands with no tick tock.
Imagine being followed the needles and the pins
and the danger of a trip out,
a death trap with every single step, a march of fear.

Imagine owning a pet, its obedience uncared for.
Imagine not hearing yourself think
and the void the mind roams,
the darkness its only comfort, muffled by tar.

Imagine if you will the deafness of silence, a missing sense.
Imagine seeing and feeling
and still being a prisoner,
captured inside a bubble of not a word, somewhat damaged.

when at last that cocaine line of light stabs deep
into eye pupil of black

and you shake your head shaky shake from
side to side wobbly wobble

an entirely different reflection with puzzling
flowered gaze wanders in

keep traffic light function from wandering out
and wave slow faraway

your fog lifting through deleted words inside
plastic world science

all by hotel hands that shake and welcome the
he inside of the me

this cover up for tomorrow time and tiny
milestones in situ

guiding things that point and pick in scabs of
scratchy scratch

and open gobbed on the spot plaster board table
of could

a yet again jigsaw piece crumbled by wheelie
bin rubber wheel

Interviewer: So Mr Baxter, where did you come up with this idea?

Mr Baxter: Well I first had the idea because I asked myself what would I need Virtual Reality for? I have everything on the account of being very rich and very well off. Other persons would use VR, which stands for Virtual Reality, as a means of escape or to live out dreams and lives they could, and never would, accomplish. For example a poor person would use the luxury programme and see what it would be like to live like me for example. A person who has lost a limb, an arm or a leg, might use the sports programme. An old person might use it to re-live childhood...and so on and so on, you get my meaning.

Interviewer: I do.

Mr Baxter: That's why I created the poor programme, although it is so much more than that. Yes, one could see what it's like to be poor, on the streets begging for money being looked at with disgust or ignored. Sleeping under rags and newspapers covered in one's own piss and shit. Scavenging bins for half eaten mouldy scraps of food thrown out by the likes of me...you know; a programme to relieve the boredom of being very rich and very well off. But one could also see what it's like to be drugged and raped, buggered and sold as a sex slave. Kept locked in a dungeon or warehouse and passed round fat sweaty men for their pleasure. There is even a secret suicide programme hidden within...hard to find but well worth it. Overdose, gun to the face, slice of the wrists...you name it, it's in there.

Interviewer: And it's proven to be very successful, sold out within days?

Mr Baxter: Indeed it has, went straight in at number one in the gaming charts and is still there after six months. Us rich people are full of culture, need and want you know...we are not just walking wallets (laughs).

Interviewer: (laughs) No, of course not (laughs). So what is next then? I hear you are working on a new programme?

Mr Baxter: I am yes. This VR will put the person into the life of an animal or a pet. You will get to experience the blade of the butcher as he slices your throat and drains your blood. Or you could experience the feeling of drowning from the inside of a plastic bag you owner has just thrown into the river. Starved, beaten, caged, forced to fight even. There is even a secret programme within this one as well.

Interviewer: Really, could you tell us or maybe even just give us a little clue?

Mr Baxter: (laughs) Well, I can't tell you but I will give you a clue..."squeal like a pig" except this time, you will be an actual pig (laughs) (pauses) (laughs) (pauses) (laughs) (laughs) (laughs) (laughs)

On the horizon

From under here I can see the horizon,
and I ask it why he did the things he did,
a father isn't supposed to do those things,
a husband isn't supposed to do those things.

From under here I can see the horizon,
and I ask it why he said what he said,
a father isn't supposed to say those words,
a husband isn't supposed to say those words.

From under here I can see the horizon,
and I ask it why he hurt when he hurt,
a father isn't supposed to hurt his love,
a husband isn't supposed to hurt his love.

From under here I can see the horizon,
and I ask it why he left when he left,
a father isn't supposed to leave his family,
a husband isn't supposed to leave his family.

On the horizon,
I ask it why,
father,
husband.

TO BE SHOUTED FROM UNDER SEVERAL TABLES OF VARIOUS SIZES AND ALL BUNCHED TOGETHER

THE ANSWER IS NOT TO BAN GUNS. THE ANSWER IS NOT TO MAKE THEM HARDER TO GET. THE ANSWER IS NOT TO CHANGE THE LAW. THE ANSWER IS MORE GUNS. THE ANSWER IS TO MAKE THEM EASIER FOR THE PUBLIC TO GET. THE ANSWER IS TO MAKE THEM MORE AFFORDABLE. THE ANSWER IS TO AMEND THE LAW AND REDUCE THE AGE A PERSON CAN GET A GUN. GUNS DEFEND PEOPLE. GUNS MAKE PEOPLE FEEL SAFE. GUNS KILL PEOPLES WHO WILL KILL YOU AND WHOM YOU CANNOT KILL IF YOU HAVEN'T GOT A GUN. THIS IS THE ANSWER.

to be whispered from under several table of various sizes and all bunched together

the answer is not to ban guns. the answer is not to make them harder to get. the answer is not to change the law. the answer is stricter gun registrations. the answer is gun control. the answer is to increase the cost of purchasing a gun. the answer is to make them only available through licensed and monitored gun shops. guns do not kill people. irresponsible and mentally unstable people who own guns kill people. this is the answer.

Alien Captain: Those fucking humans are fucking killing each other again.

Alien First Officer: Again?! What is it this time? Religion? Prejudice? Homophobia? Sport?

Alien Captain: Fuck knows...fucking idiots.

Alien First Officer: Captain...don't they get it? Don't they understand they only have one life?

Alien Captain: Seems the knob heads don't! You can tell they only use a small percentage of their brains, I mean the power of the human brain...if only they knew!

Alien First Officer: Maybe we should teach them? Show them the way.

Alien Captain: Fuck that! If you think I, or any of our race, are going down to that planet you must be as crazy as them fuckers!

Alien First Officer: Lol...good point! What do you reckon...hundred years before humanity has wiped itself out?

Alien Captain: LMFAO...more like 20-30 years...dick heads they are!

A man and a woman sit across from each other in an office. Computers and files litter each desk.

Man: How do you know if I have got any legs?
Woman: What?
Man: How do you know if I have got any legs?
Woman: What sort of question is that?
Man: A very valid question
Woman: Well, of course you have legs
Man: But how do you know?
Woman: Because you do
Man: What is your proof?
Woman: Listen, I have got a lot of work to do and I don't understand the stupid question
Man: I always arrive at the office before you...yes?
Woman: Er, yes, I suppose
Man: And I leave the office after you...yes?
Woman: Yeah so, I'm pretty sure I have seen you go make a coffee or go the toilet
Man: Have you? Have you ever seen me get up from behind this desk and walk around?
Woman: Oh come on, I must have...sometime...
Man: But have you?
Woman: My god! No I actually don't think I have
Man: So, I ask again, how do you know if I have got any legs?
Woman: Nice try...if you haven't got any legs, how do you get here in the morning and then get home in the evening?
Man: Maybe I don't. How do you know I don't stay here all day and all night?
Woman: What?
Man: How do you know I don't stay here all day and all night?
Woman: But, don't you have a family, a wife and kids?
Man: I used to...but they abandoned me here when my legs fell off
Woman: Holy shit...your legs fell off?!
Man: Yep. I went to sleep one night and the next morning, they had just fallen off
Woman: That's awful...what did the Doctors say?
Man: They said my legs had just given up, had enough and just fallen off
Woman: What about prosthetics? Have you tried them?
Man: No...it just wouldn't seem right

Woman: Well…I'm so sorry. Can I get you anything? A drink? Something to eat?
Man: Why?
Woman: Er, what do you mean why?
Man: Why are you offering to get me a drink or something to eat?
Woman: Well, because you can't get it yourself
Man: Why can't I get it myself?
Woman: Because you haven't got any legs
Man: How do you know if I haven't got any legs?
Woman: You've just told me
Man: Yeah but how do you really know?
Woman: Oh fuck off!

A man and a woman sit across from each other in an office. Computers and files litter each desk.

I'M SO FAT I HATE IT

then do something about it

I COMFORT EAT

find something else to replace it

I DON'T GET TIME TO EXERCISE

bet you get time to watch the tv...exercise in front of the tv

I HAVE NO MOTIVATION

look in the fucking mirror

I CAN'T AFFORD THE GYM

bet you can afford to order takeaway every fucking week

IT'S A CONDITION

that's a bullshit excuse

I AM JUST BIG BONED

bones are not made from fat knob head

IT'S IN MY GENES

of course it is tit face

I LOVE JUNK FOOD TOO MUCH

that's because it's designed to be loved due to its high volume of salt and sugar

I'M JUST TOO LAZY

not gonna argue with that

I'VE HAD A HARD LIFE

so have millions of other people

I'M GETTING OVER THE DEATH OF A LOVED ONE

by eating yourself to an early grave

THERE IS NOTHING WRONG WITH BEING FAT

yes it is because it can fucking kill you

I'M PERFECTLY HAPPY THE WAY I AM

no you are fucking not

(this is a song...and as it is a song, it must be sung because that's what songs get happened)

What's in the drawer?

What's in the drawer you motherfucker?
A couple of bank cards and a pair of lips sucker.
Open the drawer and let us see your shit.
It best not be a drawer full of grit.

Horns and guitar play an ungodly sound.
Give me proof that the world is round.
The conventions that we are forever bound.
Oh dear, what's this I have found?

All hail the drawer that sits inside the table from which we perform.
All hail the drawer that sits inside the table from which we are born.

What's in the drawer you funt?
Let's make a guess and have a punt.
Reach into the very back and finger feel.
Rock back and forward full of steel.

Piano and drums pound through the night.
Don't you dare run, turn back and fight.
Indeed the darkness can blot out the light.
The dead wood can no longer bite.

All hail the drawer that sits inside the table from which we dance.
All hail the drawer that sits inside the table from which we take a chance.

What's in the drawer you bitch?
Pens and pencils to make us all rich.
Photographs existing when the drawer is ajar.
My mind is gone away so far away far.

Voices and saxophone wail over my bones.
My ears distorted shaped like cones.
The drawer clatters full of stones.
What is it you sing over that there telephones?

All hail the drawer that sits inside the table from which we live.
All hail the drawer that sits inside the table from within our soul we give.

IT IS VERY DARK UNDERNEATH HERE...

YOU DO KNOW THAT YOU WILL DIE SOME DAY?
YOU ARE NOT INDEED IMMORTAL DESPITE THINKING IT.
ONE DAY, ALL THAT YOU WERE WILL BE GONE.
ONE DAY, ALL THAT YOU DID WILL BE FORGOTTEN.
ONE DAY, ALL THAT YOU TOUCHED WILL BE LEFT COLD.

SAD THOUGHT ISN'T IT? MAKES YOU FEEL VERY SMALL DOESN'T IT? MAKES YOU QUESTION THE POINT OF IT ALL IF ULTIMATELY, IT ALL GOES AWAY. THE WORLD WILL GO AWAY. WE ARE ALL ALONE. THERE IS NO LIGHT COMING FOR US....

WHICH IS WHY IT IS VERY DARK UNDERNEATH THE TABLE.
WHICH IS WHY IT IS VERY SCARY BEYOND THE TABLE.

SMALL MINDED PERSON: I DON'T WANT TO LEAVE

LARGE MINDED PERSON: BUT YOU HAVE TO

SMALL MINDED PERSON: BUT I AM FRIGHTENED OUT THERE

LARGE MINDED PERSON: SO AM I...

At the end of the day, why should I? I got a roof over my head, a nice bit of lush carpet to sit on, a heater on one side of me and an open window on the other. I reach around to the left and I can find my books and some toilet paper. I reach around to my right and I can find storage space and my toothbrush. As long as I keep my teeth clean...I don't need a shower. If I need to go to do number one, I got a water bottle. If I need to go number two, there is a bin in the corner of the room. I don't shit in the bin...god man, I'm not barbaric. No, I shit in some toilet paper, wrap it up and throw it in the bin. See this little stove here, behind my back; I use it to boil my piss and then re-drink it...always thinking about recycling and the environment.

Of course people come to visit me. They speak to me through the window...after they move the chair out of the way of course. Although I don't get too many visitors really. Not sure why, maybe it's the smell...can be a bit pungent...the bin overflows fairly quickly. And maybe me being naked puts people off sometimes. Well, what do I need clothes for? Just get in the way...it's not like I got all the space in the world under here!

But I would never leave my home for all the money in the world. It's cosy, safe and warm...what more could you ever want in life...what more could you ever want in life... what more could you ever want in life...what more could you ever want in life... what more could you ever want in life...what more could you ever want in life... what more could you ever want in life...what more could you ever want in life... what more could you ever want in life...what more could you ever want in life... what more could you ever want in life...what more could you ever want in life... what more could you ever want in life...what more could you ever want in life... what more could you ever want in life...what more could you ever want in life... what more could you ever want in life...what more could you ever want in life... what more could you ever want in life...what more could you ever want in life... what more could you ever want in life...what more could you ever want in life... what more could you ever want in life...what more could you ever want in life... what more could you ever want in life...what more could you ever want in life... what more could you ever want in life...what more could you ever want in life... what more could you ever want in life...what more could you ever want in life... what more could you ever want in life...what more could you ever want in life... what more could you ever want in life...what more could you ever want in life... what more could you ever want in life...what more could you ever want in life... what more could you ever want in life...what more could you ever want in life... what more could you ever want in life...what more could you ever want in life... what more could you ever want in life...what more could you ever want in life... what more could you ever want in life...what more could you ever want in life... what more could you ever want in life...what more could you ever want in life... what more could you ever want in life...what more could you ever want in life... what more could you ever want in life...what more could you ever want in life... what more could you ever want in life...what more could you ever want in life... what more could you ever want in life...what more could you ever want in life... what more could you ever want in life...what more could you ever want in life... what more could you ever want in life...what more could you ever want in life... what more could you ever want in life...what more could you ever want in life... what more could you ever want in life...what more could you ever want in life... what more could you ever want in life...what more could you ever want in life... what more could you ever want in life...what more could you ever want in life... what more could you ever want in life...what more could you ever want in life... what more could you ever want in life...what more could you ever want in life... what more could you ever want in life...what more could you ever want in life... what more could you ever want in life...what more could you ever want in life...oh god, I've wasted my life.

we, the puppet

we dangle
and we hang
wasting away
observers in our own demise
the curtain
ready to close
bringing with it
only darkness
a nothingness
of regret
of loss
and time has ended
and it's too late
death chokes out our last breath
company for the residents of those who stayed under the table

when tick tock of pointy hands spells end of
pushed out chest flutter flutter

and you weep like a little child who's just lost his mummy
in supermarket rush

an eerie wave of empty mug feeling brings with it
dregs that swim and laugh

keep at distance those shadows that love and dance
around blank sorry state

your fight inside gut of twist and brain of mush
antiques onwards

all because your walls vein of graffiti and eraser words

this substance sticky and black coating your very
being of soul

guiding maggots to feast consume the waterhole happy
goodness

and open a diseased hole that will never heal sway
grass seed

a wave of victory for daddy dad dad situated through
rhapsody limbo

This is how I see it.

I don't want to be told what I can and cannot do in my own house. I worked hard to get this house the way I want it. I don't want to be told who I can let into my house. I decide the person or persons suitable enough to step foot in my house. If I make something in my house and I want to sell it, then I will. If no one wants to buy what I have made, then I will make something else. I will not give up and risk losing my house. If my neighbours need help, then I will help them. Life will go on. The Earth will keep turning. Space will still be vast. We will all die...very single one of us, one day, soon maybe? Maybe not. 24/06/16.

Rikki

Came home one day high on speed,
the look of little Rikki was one of need,
kicking him to the ground, she moves to the sink,
why does she do these things, why do you think?

Forcing his head back, the liquid goes down,
all is heard is a whisper, a single sound,
all is seen is a word written on his head,
"fetch me my sherbet my little one" is all she said.

Laid out in a star, why was I crucified so?
Mummy I love you, it's time to go.

I sat down on the bus, one side was reserved for the old, the other, for the wondrous.

A middle aged woman with an ankle tattoo and a black eye sat in front of me, her expression was one of pain and hate. When our eyes collided, she stared me down with a smile and a wink.

An old man with one of those startled looks on his face sat opposite me.

Behind me, a small child watched in awe as the world rushed by and her mother failed to keep her still and silent.

Heavy breathing came from the drunk who slept in the back corner.

A teenager was lost in his own musical fantasy as tinny tunes came from the ear-plug headphones he was wearing; I strained to listen.

Two giant white fluffy perms waddled on, and sat in front of the startled man, lost in conversation about shopping they didn't even pause for breath.

I looked at my watch and caressed the scars the strap was hiding. It had been two years since my failed suicide attempt and I wondered if she would notice. Could she handle the truth if I told her?

The caged driver pulled into my stop and as I got off, an anorak backpacker flashed his bus pass like someone from the FBI and proceeded to sit down where I had been sitting...nice and warm.

I watched and waved as the 395 grumbled off leaving me with an air of exhaust fumes, and, keeping my hands in my pockets, I realised my journey had only just began.

He was on his third coffee and second saffron cake. A single daffodil decorated the iffy table affecting balance and temper. What had been called in as a simple affray on a scruffy Suffolk morning had turned into his most difficult case. A member of staff offered him more caffeine, miffed he accepted giving Jefferson, the name tag revealed, a muffled naff-off stare. The drowning out of traffic by a chaffinch took him back to his morning; the duffel bag full of snuff, the blind officer stuffed into a coffin, the Staffordshire sniffer dog suffocated and stiff, the biff, the boff, the scuffle...it was an effort to stay focused.

He paused.

Could he afford the toffee waffles that caught his eye on the buffet menu or should he scoff the stroganoff soufflé? Suffice to say, he suffered over them both, yet his affair for the Jaffa muffin became his official decision. His eyes caught a whiff of who shuffled around the diner. A boffin with the biggest quiff was faffing around with a truffle. A young couple full of affection buffered each other with love and affinity. The gaffer chased out a buffoon with a fluffy dog wearing a baffled look.

He paused.

He was suddenly vibrating. Fluffing about for his phone un-affected by the riff-raff enclosed around him, he answered...it was the office, it was piffle, and it was time to go.

Speaking to Strangers (imagine that)

To possess little or nothing, imagine
being without a means of subsistence?
A state of being poor is a state of need, imagine,
huddled in a ball of inadequacy?

To feel cold and inferior, imagine,
a personal anthem of deficiency?
The meagreness of many or the one, imagine,
the illusion of basic necessities?

To suffer inside a rich man's pocket, imagine,
own less in your own country?
A supposed great Britain, imagine,
the ignorance of helping others first?

To be aware and do nothing, imagine,
the viewed appearance of a stain?
Together as a band of pipers, imagine,
if we spoke to strangers?

Dreamer: Do I see bells in the distance, hear eyes emotion stare?
Non-Dreamer: I can't see further than my own hand, but who cares?
Dreamer: Time ticks away at its own breath like a whisper, a whisper through the air.
Non-Dreamer: I need a new battery for my watch, life is so unfair.
Dreamer: A line, a simple line forms in my mind and I am free, at last I am free.
Non-Dreamer: Get the kettle on, let's enjoy a nice cup of tea.
Dreamer: I drown in music, my lungs fill with sound, it stops.
Non-Dreamer: It's time for the soaps, lots and lots and lots.
Dreamer: A single note touches my lips, to be or not to be? Maybe? Probably!
Non-Dreamer: There are only the four walls around me, all I can see.
Dreamer: I'm on a swing now, strings take me higher.
Non-Dreamer: This dreamer is a big fat stupid liar.
Dreamer: Strings and oboe, clarinet and cello, violins and violas.
Non-Dreamer: Thinking he is all that, thinking he has that buzz.
Dreamer: Voices! I can touch the voices with my heart, my empty heart.
Non-Dreamer: Get ready everyone for an almighty fart.
Dreamer: And it fills. With inspiration...and hope.
Non-Dreamer: I love my life. Dreamer you say? Nope.

this poem is untitled

blue flowers prickle, sting, pain
joy of life smiles from above
shadows prance about springtime
rain
trophies walk by, won by love

a genies lamp erupts into song
carpet babies crawl on air
the piece of string so long
medusa's snakes...her hair

random lines make random noise
like bells from below
home the back bring boys
green is the colour...go!

Neighbours...(everybody needs good neighbours) (depending where you live)

Balls bounce off weathered bricks (I fucking hate the noise and the thud thud of stupid balls striking the walls of stone...go play in a fucking park on fucking grass)
Parents serenade their children's names (screaming and shouting for their brats to "GET IN" or screeching their names like a squealing fucking pig)
Pets taken for walkies fetching sticks (shitting on the pavement, barking at anything that dares look at it and attacking the innocent)
Knock and run amongst other games (harassing the elderly or disadvantaged with a dare and a pathetic brave face).

An old timer waddles out for food (half starving, abandoned by the system and left to rot alone and scared)
An over timer plods home for bed (the need to work longer hours to cover the bills in a country run by the rich)
A teen on the corner undercover of mood (undercover of drugs and criminal scumbag hiding away a face of disgrace)
A girl whose life is a mirror unfed (abused and used, a plaything for the special uncle sharing with his special friends).

Taxi's indicate it's time to go out (look at them getting pissed, picking fights and ruining the nights of the others)
Yet parked cars indicate it's time to stay in (or be stolen by the supposed trust worthy who live yards from you)
Pushbikes race by with kids on doubt (hanging round the shop corner to spread fear and hatred into anyone and anything)
Drunks zig zag on legs of thin (their only joy in life is also their one way ticket out of life drowning in a sea of puke and blood).

This is the view from my abode (although I wish it wasn't)
After months, weeks, day labour (I just want to see green)
Litters of signs scattered and sold (maybe someday)
For better or worse these are neighbours (these aren't...these are scum fucks).

(written whilst living in Cornbrook)

when threat of green green grass to be turned
into concrete and ash

and feeling of “here we go again” twists now in fat
blubbery belly

an intense rush of dictionary words officiate over
eyes of hate

keep blinking to see the many possible probable palpable
horizons

your past now likely to come full circle and
swallow your present

all down to greed and gas need a transfusion the bones of
the earth

this cheek of humanity in charge turned to face far
far away

guiding machines and thumpy thump to do their job
regardless

and destroy a sea of life swaying with a breathing
distinctness

a sad day for the truly soulful spirits whose hearts splayed
open wide

The privilege of time

Tick tock clicks the piece, observing and counting,
Our lives dictated by the workings of time;
Amongst cogs, gears and the welfare of hands,
Stretching out, pointing and striking, never stopping.

The watch of youth becoming the grandfather clock,
As alarms wake us and buzzers free us.
Minutes can last hours, vice versa the deceiving seconds,
A lifetime of "where did it all go?"

Shadows expand and shrink, grow then wither,
Colours bloom before reverting to black and white
And as we speak, moments are a wasting, marching;
An army of forward determination.

Any possible pasts swallowed and lost, a feeling,
Of hanging on in timid desperation; what side?
That catches up with us all, no mercy, no escape,
This is the privilege of time.

Scene – a man and a woman are lying on top of a table having sex. There is another man under the table reading a book.

Man: Aaaahh

Woman: Oooohh

Man: Aaaahh

Woman: Oooohh

Man: Aaaahh

Woman: Oooohh

Man: Aaaahh

Woman: Oooohh

Man: Aaaahh

Woman: Oooohh

Man: Aaaahh

Woman: Oooohh

Man: Aaaahh

Woman: Oooohh

Man: Aaaahh

Woman: Oooohh

Man: Aaaahh

Woman: Oooohh

Man: Aaaahh

Woman: Oooohh

Man: Aaaahh

Woman: Oooohh

Man: Aaaahh

Woman: Oooohh

Man: Aaaahh

Woman: Oooohh

Man: Aaaahh

Woman: Oooohh

Man: Aaaahh

Woman: Oooohh

Man: Aaaahh

Woman: Oooohh

Man: Aaaahh

Woman: Oooohh

Man: Aaaahh

Woman: Oooohh

Man: Aaaahh

Woman: Oooohh

Man: Aaaahh

Woman: Oooohh

Man: Aaaahh

Woman: Oooohh

Man: Aaaahh

Woman: Oooohh

Man: Aaaahh

Woman: Oooohh

Man: Aaaahh

Woman: Oooohh

Man under the table: Can you please pack it in; I am trying to read this book!!

My ring bound pad begins to fill with words

I sit peering at my off coloured feet, cold and ugly they hang like dead fish floating in a polluted sea. My pants are flailed, old and black, worn and tight, cheap and nasty...they just cling. I take a swig from a cracked glass, cheap lemonade irritates my throat and fizzes as it eats away at my teeth, itching, and coating.

Ideas live and die in an instant. Worlds created and destroyed in a heartbeat. Lines written and erased in a glance.

I look up and out from under this table as shadows swap sides and time does the marathon...how long have I been under here? My mind strains, my bladder gives me orders and it is then that I enter the zone...at the most inconvenient moment, my ring bound pad begins to fill with words...horrors...

Eyes like black holes
Breathing pounding drums
Yet screams ring true
Of horrors so real

Stomach torn open
Movement restricted
Pain extreme erotic
The flesh comes
Dark, sexy, red

Horrors, horrors
Possibilities endless
Torture imaginative
Creativity free
Suffering fucks me
Oh please fuck me
Inside out, inside out
Make me come
Make me bleed

...horrors, the pen seems possessed, willing itself to fill the blank page with whatever words it feels like. I let it. I dare not stop it. I feel it take control.

Like a fat slug, I slide out from under the table and attempt to stand up with some grace and dignity. There is none as I amble my carcass to the toilet and give my bladder the relief it wants. Behind me, I hear my ring bound pad begin to fill with more words.

Fragile

Tears fall into the infinite – slow, fragile.
Your eyes search for hope, I cannot give.
We knew no-one was on our side, why?
Isn't the point of love exactly that – the point!
I brush your white skin for the last time
and hold you to my heart. You listen
wishing to capture every beat left in me.
An impossible wish in an impossible dream.
Yet you try...and you pray...and you almost succeed.
Almost.
But I slip.
And I fall into the infinite – slow, fragile.

I am sitting in the garden...in the wooden arbour to be absolutely precise. I have a fairly big garden, maybe around 100 feet in length and 70 in width. There are various plants and roses littered around the border (barely alive) as well as tiny fences no more than a ruler in height separating the grass from the path and stone filled court yard. There are only 4 houses (converted barns) in our little section but there are no neighbours left in them anymore – sad really.

I sit listening to a soundtrack of thumping with a landscape of concrete and a huge drill fucking the Earth mere yards from the garden. It never used to be this way. For miles, all I could see was farmer's fields, forests of trees and hills rolling in the distance.

All dead now.

The buzz of animal and bird life has been wiped out and the colours of nature are nothing more than a grey splodge – sad really.

Every day, I feel the house shift and move. The fracking drill splitting and cracking the foundations of the land and its surroundings. The water has been poisoned, the air is filthy and the heat...even on cold days...is unbearable. I can only use bottled water, stay outside for about 15 minutes at a time and have fans on pretty much all the time...especially during the night time.

What once was a gorgeous, open, peaceful area is now a horrible, suffocating, busy mess – sad really.

But I will not move. I will be defiant. I will try my best to protect what I have and keep it alive and relevant. Yes, the neighbours were bought out, at a damn high price as well, but I will not be bought out. There is more to this life than money...there is integrity and pride.

Still – sad really.

I don't feel so well. I have a banging headache and my bones ache...bet that's what the Earth is feeling. Raped, pillaged, violated and destroyed – sad really.

Sad really – sad really – sad really – sad really – sad really – sad really – sad really – sad really – sad....

A scratch on a record

I knew I could never go back there
An advent of darkness now before me
As dust filled words follow empty voices
Whispers of regret and faith, no more.

For to go back there would be
Harder than it is to be here
A kind reminder of a sin committed
Littered by actions of self-harm
And left with a curse of memory
Of what I gave up and extinguished.

The coolness and safety of the night
The life and uncertainty of the day
Touch, taste, smell, sight, feelings.

The building crescendo of music.

Yet fear hold dear
Ruled my excuse for existence
And condemned me governing my decision
A certain finality twisted
One more day of regret.

A scratch on a record.

the man who found what he never had

The man who found what he never had
(or woman – we are not sexist here)
Was finally proved wrong 'bout good and bad
(although there is all the stuff in between)
Swimming through time on a face of sad
(can you swim through time on any face?)
Turn that frown upside down he wasn't mad
(or she – we are not sexist here)

Hellish thoughts burning screaming in despair
(obviously)
The mask of hate jealous ripped and bare
(we all wear masks)
Bars of his cage bent destroyed no care
(or hers – we are not sexist here)
Inside voices shut out shut up so unaware
(basically, just keep them voices quiet)

The mirror image would smile back
(be a bit freaky though)
And eventually that would be that
(wait, it would be all over)
His heart would be peaceful rested at
(or hers – we are not sexist here)
A silent mind muted song sacked
(actually sacked?)

But the man who found what he never had
(or woman – we are not sexist here)
Who was finally proved 'bout good and bad
(yeah but there is all the stuff in between)
Knew how it was gonna end since he was a lad
(or a lass – we are not sexist here)
In black and white on a ring bound pad
(a ring bound pad that begins to fill with words).

The white feathers of a majestic swan are bright against a deep breath, a dark voice. Once young, now old...a lifetime of moments, some lived amongst the sundown, some dead within the cemetery.

A time recorded in pulp and documents is a canvas of work now finished and rewarded with a pat on the back and a forgotten "well done." One hand embraced the innocence while the other shunned our freedom.

Further down the spiral, is it denial or realization? A remix or a shake-up...this withered truth. Fewer years ahead than gone...is this fact or fiction? For what was it all worth and for where did it fly to?

Best focus on the hole left behind, this retirement filled with golf, pets and lie ins. Something for everyone to look forward to...the epiphany of a life wasted or the epiphany of a life celebrated?

And so, the white feathers of a majestic swan - will they flounder within the dregs of age...the oil? Or will they eclipse those moments with mighty wings, their silhouette across the lone sundown disappearing within the busy cemetery.

Or now, finally...live a little.

Trust: Hello, my name is trust. What is your name?

Naïve: Hello trust, my name is naïve. What do you do?

Trust: Well, I make people believe in me and what I say. What do you do?

Naïve: I believe in anything and everything as the truth. I also think that everything in the world is all ok.

Trust: But you do know that everything in the world is not ok.

Naïve: Of course everything in the world is ok...this is what I believe.

Trust: Trust me, everything in the world is not ok...my name is trust, believe in me.

Naïve: But trust is the one thing I don't believe in and the one thing I know isn't ok.

Trust: But why? That doesn't make sense at all.

Naïve: Anything and everything told me not to trust trust.

Trust: What?

Anything & Everything: That's right, we told naïve not to trust trust but to believe in us instead because we are the truth and we are ok.

Naïve: That's right...and I stick to my guns.

My Guns: That's right, naïve sticks with me.

Trust: This is crazy...are you all mad...

Crazy: Someone call me?

Trust: Who are you?

Crazy: I am crazy...I view the world in a very different way to everyone else.

Everyone else: It's true...he really does.

Trust: What is going on?

Naïve: Wow...so many people here.

Table: Would you lot bugger off from out under me, I got a lot of standing still to do and I can't do that with all this chitter chatter.

Chitter Chatter: Don't blame me, I just got here!

Let's dance and sing and pretend it's all going to be ok

✓ Because we are all talk and no action

- We won't support the ones that have done so much for us because we are all talk and no action and because we are selfish and stupid

- We will just sit on our fat asses and complain with words to ourselves

- Hypocrites are we, yes we are

- Doesn't really affect us, we have a backup plan

- So we will screw over the ones who don't have a backup plan because at the end of the day, we don't really care for them despite all the things they have done for us through the nature of their heart

✓ So basically fuck them as long as we are ok, fuck them right in the ear...

when you sit and question those that supposed to
care for you stroke stroke

and smell their falsehoods from across miles
and miles of even smellier fields

an intolerable smile shatters like jigsaw pieces
destined to never fit

keep sake for future reference of fool for me
fool for you

your bullshit scraping with claw like sausage
fingers of meat

all in plain view visible in the walls by the
wolves snarling

this disappointing traverse of humanity so
prevalent amongst "friends"

guiding with them a line of following puppets
destined to be the number zero

and snigger to themselves as if them got one over
on the you

a fact so far from the actuality it becomes a
funny funny of divinity

you: I'm going to ignore you until I need something
me: I don't need anything from you
you: but that's ok because I am allowed to ignore you because of the life I lead
me: it's the life you choose to lead
you: and I choose to stand a yard away from you and not even look into your eyes
me: you do that...I know the type of person you are
you: but when I need something, I will do everything in my power to be all over you like a rash
me: I have noticed that is the way it goes
you: and then, when I don't need you, I will discard you like a used tissue
me: because that is what I mean to you
you: you are nothing to me
me: nothing
you: a means to an end
me: means to an end?
you: I put up with you because I need to use you
me: you don't care
you: I don't care...I mean, why would I?
me: care?
you: yes...look at you...pathetic
me: so basically, what you are saying is that I mean nothing to you unless you need something?
you: yes
me: and even then, you put up with me because you have no choice?
you: exactly correct
me: are you sure you aren't jealous?
you: ....
me: of the life I lead and the person I am and what I do
you: ....
me: thought so.

Those who

I can see from under this table
that there are those who
want to reach down and pull me out
from under this table.

Yet I can also see
that there are those who
want to bury me with their shit
brick me in under this table.

At times from what I hear
that there are those who
want to leave me alone
walk past me under this table.

A couple of moments I feel
that there are those who
spit on me
kick me as I lay under this table.

Yet in the end, from under this table I know
that there are those who
like me don't even care
forever I am under this table.

This man...my father

Sometimes I just sit here and think. I wonder what it would be like to feel my mother's arms around me again.

I miss her so much.

Yet I still cannot mourn her properly.

Is it because I still refuse to believe she is really gone? Even after 15 years.

Or is it because she really isn't gone?

Other people pat me on the back and say "well done" or "you are a good man" but I couldn't save my own mother. I don't deserve a well done...I never deserve a well done.

Because the guilt runs through my veins. The loss burns away my soul. The hatred beats against my heart.

And then there was him, this man...my father.

A man should protect and love his wife. A man should never leave her side and be the best he can for her and their children. A man isn't meant to abuse and hurt.

This man...my father.

The lies, the pain, the bullshit.

This man...my father.

He had it all. In the palm of his hands he held my mother, her petals so bright and colourful, ripe to be cared for and marvelled at.

Instead he plucked. Instead he fucked. Instead she cried. Instead she died.

This man...my father.

He lost it all and in doing so, took away so much. His legacy is a damage that can never be undone and a flower that was meant to blossom but instead withered.

This man...my father.

I am part of the human race
We murder and rape each other
We abuse
lock away
cook and eat
the animals we share this planet with
And, speaking of the planet we live on
we pollute the shit out of it
and generally fuck that up as well.

If we don't agree on each other's beliefs
then we will kill and blow ourselves up
Our superiority means
we are above the animals
and as such
have no respect
or real love
for them
The earth is nothing more
than a dumping ground
for our shit
and
to be drilled into
to run our machines.

We share no equality
colour, gender, age…fuck it
Let's destroy animals into extinction
use their coats and bones
as playthings
Wipe out the forests
piss in the seas
extract fossil fuels…

…we have even managed to fill space with junk.

I am part of the human race
and I am embarrassed
disgusted
disgraced
and fucking furious
to be part of the human race…

…and so should you.

The Gecko suite (half finished...never to be finished) – based on an original idea by Steven Gibson

Gecko

A twisted gut rips in a crimson flash,
the darkness that follows, brief and quiet,
then that sudden drop beyond a lost earth,
followed by a rush of confused convulsions,
and the welcoming claws of hell that awaits.

Clouds of fire glow and blind,
their thunder screams of the young,
as acid rain of dark independence,
strips any grave wisdom of peace.
The blackening comfort long gone,
snapping tormentors in its place,
their poisoned smiles bleed horror,
their poisoned laughs bleed hate.
Deranged faces grit welcoming gums,
as crushed teeth gnaw and shatter,
a damned expression of intensity,
Gecko's decent into a mirrored void.
Past walls of stitched flesh,
and over stinking rotten bile,
its arms reach and snap away,
deep down the trauma hounds pace.
The chasm of serenity opens,
its silent pain deforms and burns,
its brief awe strips the insides out,
and the ground a shadow casts.
Slammed hard with cursed heart,
the damning is about to begin,
a now eternity of soul torture,
a now eternity of paying the price...

...and yet in the body left behind,
a now eternity of worth burns an angel,
a now eternity of residence takes place,
a now eternity of layered forgiveness is to be earned...

Fallen

...pain

ripped............................feathers, the blood stained feathers.

Float away

are lost

to be earned, won back.

Falling with sweet rain, dropping through forked lightning,

my target chosen
my task simple
or so I thought..Gecko!

...a twisted gut rips in a crimson flash,
the brightness that follows, timeless and deafening,
then that sudden rise beyond a lost hell,
followed by a rush of confused convulsion,
and the welcoming claws of life that await.

Dreams

My white wings grew back different.
Black and full of a hateful pain.

I sat next to God itself at one time.
Trusted and full of a wise head.

A twisted gut rips in a crimson flash.
The brightness that follows, oh so bright.

The bells that sealed my fate bled.
My fellow brothers wept with disguise.

A punishment to run the punished.
A kingdom overrun and kept at bay.

I miss my white wings.
They grew back differently.

My ignorance no longer bottled.
My defiance no longer silenced.

My fall from grace the first.
My name now said with fear.

A distant machine keeps Gecko alive.
Only in body, his soul with me.

The halls of heaven stunning in detail.
A peace surrounds its walls.

I will earn back my white wings.
Through forgiveness through Gecko.

A distant machine beeps closer.
I feel my mind drifting away.

The people's spit drips on my face.
As I feel frightened for the very first time.

My memories now locked in my nightmares.
A final irony shakes me awake.

Focusing on very different surroundings.
A recognition in a hospital.

The pain in my stomach tingles.
The bruises in my soul purple.

How did I get here? Who am I?

A Memory Taken For Granted

Staring at the ceiling backed into the corner,
a blankness ticks away in mourning,
the missing jigsaw pieces lost or disguised,
a memory taken for granted now the refugee.

Looking around for those all important clues,
leaves me orphaned and misplaced,
a lone stranger in a holiday inn,
a memory taken for granted now the lodger.

My vocal questions met with disdain,
any protest an empty and feeble gesture,
unknown reasons or explanations silenced,
a memory taken for granted, now the ignored.

The twisted gut that ripped in a crimson flash,
what reasoning for this black thing,
is death picking at me in pieces of eights,
a memory taken for granted now the targeted.

Fatigue overcomes the pat present fear,
sleep drowns this bodies need for answers,
faces watch me drift into oblivions pet,
a memory taken for granted now the nightmares…

Mona

The cigarette the childhoods end.
A forced guilt no longer shared.
Blue smoke forms a silver ring.
And surrounds this death in shadow.
This Mona my devious addiction.
Blind to all but your soul.
Your cursed beauty irrelevant to me.

The cigarette the childhoods end.
A smell of adultery worn with arrogance.
Blue aura writes its own confession.
And a smoking gun its own priest.
This Mona my confused tears.
Blind to your lifeless dead eyes.
Your cursed body flaccid over me.

Beautiful? Always.

And deep down Gecko crawls.
And deep down Gecko begs.
And deep down Gecko screams.
And deep down Gecko suffers.

And deep down his soul is slit and drained.
And deep down the clinging poison chokes.
And deep down decaying laughter brings sickness.
And deep down trapped eyes are forced to see.
And deep down the throbbing sound draws near.
And deep down a wall of tortured hems him in.
And deep down spinning the undertow of hate.
And deep down the trauma hounds stand guard.

And deep down Gecko knows.
And deep down Gecko succumbs.
And deep down Gecko wishes.
And deep down Gecko's hell.

An effect lasted

...net even Mona's beauty could save her,
her dress forever wet, forever stained,
the first of many: an effect lasted.

My eyesight altered through darkness forever,
blind to any please of forgiveness and drunk,
drunk on the pitiful stink in innocence
of the weak, of the ordinary, of the young,
for next was Mona's boyish lover...
bitter to say,
angry to think,
a repulsed voice,
my victim to control.

What is revenge? What is revenge?
Revenge is a hole.
Revenge gets deeper.
revenge sucks you in.
Revenge has no light at the end of the tunnel.
(A tunnel I ripped from the earth,
smashing my knuckles upon cold rock.)

Oh I made him suffer, this boyish lover,
keeping him awake, everything to take,
his equipment first, boiling my blood thirst,
a drug of madness, a cocktail of the best,
melting off his feet, feeding him his own meat,
a surgery of insides out, irreversible damage no doubt,
loving the mind games, cutting off precious veins,
till a shell was left, a hunk at best,
which I buried aware, and all was fair,
my art to be mastered, an effect lasted.

when you find yourself suffering from moon
madness and goose call

and a few words connects beyond our
depiction of space and space

an internal spark brings with it rage of flame once
thought extinguished forever

keep pretending the external is all hunky dory
and swimmingly fab

your truth afraid to be spoken and exposed to the
masses

all because of the ties we bind ourselves both
material and ethereal

this exaggeration of facts almost apes the lost art
of the silent age

guiding me on an inevitable outcome in lines
of red scratchy scratch

and what's left but a frightened shell shivering
under a table of wood

a weeping soul caught in between the head
and the heart

Only now do I see
a hole inside of me
it weeps constantly
this hole inside of me
begging for mercy
a need to be free...

...do you see?

Feather touches skin (part 1 – start) H.R.

...cooling skin and hearts in sheets of rain,
quieting the thunder of a heart,
joining the souls of the lost,
quenching the desires and encompassing fallen beings,

Surrendering under words and stolen breaths,
and locking a stare swirling with a wanton release,
dangerous yet beautiful,
taken to the edge and pushed further on...

...until souls collide and tides break under a sea of possibilities,
beyond sanity and feeling
a light becomes free. two becomes one and an ending there will never be,
entangled nine humming,
sweet surrender under emotion,

insides out,
racing blood,
thrashing beats...a submission of each other,
heavy breaths,
and beating hearts we connect
and are taken,
swept and shipwrecked away from the mundane
to a rush of endless storms wrapped in tangled arms

blushing cheeks,
they lay spellbound and mesmerized,
his storm found in her eyes,
they drip as fallen rain
as lips brush and skin melts,
fingers carve through silky hair
and limbs tangle a waltz...

we weave in and out of mouths and tongues,
the way we slide,
kiss, glide,
a dance our bodies embrace,
wanting everything on offer,
pushing limits, positions,
switching, swapping...no stopping,
a relentless onslaught of fire and sweat...

(mmm naughty)
skin breaks, nails down back,
a slow slide of fingers searching for eyes to lock
and lips to kiss,
melting into puddles of you

the hint of salt gives way to the rush of sugar,
the sharp breath as pain gives way to pleasure
and our motions slows to a crawl,
building, building, building...circling,
a rush of need to pierce the silence with a kiss of blush.

Warm rolls of pleasure wash over the fear of pain,
locked deeply embedded,
tucked beneath your bones,
tensing muscles, twisting nerves,
every inch of skin explored,
every fibre of being kissed,
every moment had – eager to be had again...

a mirrored feeling darkness cannot taint

skin melts
as souls mingle in an ink splattered affair of hearts,
where bodies lay in puddles
from mouths and bodies twisted in raw passion,

time has now power,
the moment has been and will be again
as spent vessels reach out and trace lines
if delicate grace carving each other
with words of poetry and shattered hearts

...I would pick up the pieces and sew them with my mouth in soft kisses
and long awaited releases,

a jigsaw revealing forever captured pictures...
destined to be splintered and pieced back together
through verse and whispered tongues.

broken always finds broken

Finding a pattern through this fragmented life,
our own fractured light becomes tortured and lost,
its shards cut deep opening up once healed scars,
and spilling out come words tangled in blood and ink.

Separated, across clouds and starlight we write,
the only illumination in the darkness cast,
our shadows tainted with a rapture of pain
harvested by wings of bone and sharpened claw.

It digs into our soul and blackens our mind,
tears apart foundations built from a supposed trust,
a failed love imprinted throughout our being
is now the hated guide we tether ourselves to.

There is no freedom and time cannot save us,
we are forever locked in silent self-torture,
the punishment decided by our inner imprint
is deemed an absolute necessity and deserved so.

Yet somehow, broken always finds broken,
keeping alight the shine buried deep within,
but the cruel irony brings with it a fresh hurt,
the melancholy loss of a love never to be.

A conversation takes place between the heart and the head:

Heart: I must follow what I feel
Head: No, you must use judgment and logic
Heart: But there is no such thing as logic when it comes to love
Head: Then you will make rash decisions
Heart: They will be decisions made from instinct and passion
Head: You cannot view all the facts, quantify all the variables or plan for all the outcomes that way
Heart: Nor would I want to...isn't love a journey of exploration?
Head: Love is a journey of looking after someone, putting food on the table and keeping them safe
Heart: But it is also as much to do with an inner and outer connection, the pull between two lovers
Head: I do not believe in love for I cannot see it or explain it
Heart: Does that go for everything you cannot see or explain?
Head: Yes
Heart: Then you are an idiot
Head: Yes, I know
Heart: Ok, well let me try and explain it for you
Head: Good luck
Heart: Within us all, we have love. It will grow and it will learn. Feed off and consume the likes of art and music, poetry and nature, and most critically, the people we meet. Sometimes, our love will become damaged and hurt by the actions of those very people we meet. It will know fear, pain and treachery...
Head: How can something not seen *feel* something as powerful as fear, pain and treachery?
Heart: Because love exists in the realms of those very emotions. You can't see fear, pain or treachery when you feel them?
Head: Ok, good point
Heart: So, as I was saying, our love will become damaged but it will also become enlightened and connect with others who love...reach out and touch them regardless of distance, space or even time...
Head: That's impossible
Heart: Nothing is impossible, especially when it comes to love. It conquers all...transcends all...saves all...
Soul: I'm just gonna jump in here...love can be twisted, love can be false, love can be drained, love can be given yet not received...love is not absolute

Heart: What? Of course it is, it is...

Soul: No...listen. Beyond what the head thinks and the heart feels lies me...the soul. I am not a thing. Love is a thing, a feeling. I am light and heat, I am fire and ice, I am everything and nothing...I am forever. And once in a thousand lifetimes do I merge with another...become one and complete...the way home...

Head: You've both given me a headache...

I thought the words we spoke were only meant for each other? The poetry we exchanged seemed to be only for our souls to feed from?

I thought I was special. I thought we connected. I thought...

But I was wrong.
I am always wrong.
I was let down.
I am always let down.

Deep down, I will always be alone. A fool am I, nothing am I, storm was me, fire was me, gone...lost...ash...

Some words need to be said
some truths need to be exposed
some pain needs to be felt
sometimes a need needs.

easy for death...

…a death that could come easily for how can one love someone else if they don't love themselves?

They can't.
Simple as that.

If you don't know love for yourself, you cannot know love for someone else…

Feather touches skin (part 2 – end) H.R.

Standing still, their eyes wanted nothing more than to undress their pulsating bodies, their breaths mirrored in pulses chased with hungry eyes they chase. Like animals, they circle each other pulling off the restrictions and revealing naked body and soul, a raw ignited flesh bared and stroked...fingers longing down skin, traced with lust and teased with a softness only words can portray. Whispering deep within what is about to happen, the pleasure about to be met, a whisper of poetry drenched in sheets and stolen breathes, spread across paper and displayed...an endless book written by tormented beings separated yet so close.

So close, they can taste their tongues as they dance in each other's mouths, they can smell the scent of them held between the need and air, intoxicating each other's minds and hearts bringing with it a heat...a flame unbound as their mouths unlock and she bares her neck to him. Taste encountered. Spilling breathes against skin, pressed against the flames they ignite and as he kisses her softly, her slender neck offered to him as he entangles his fingers in her hair and tugs ever so slightly melting under fingers she whimpers, pressed to his exhale.

She wraps her arms and legs around him tight as every inch of her neck is tasted, tickled by lips she moans against his skin, her teeth pulling at lobes and gentle licks, he gently kisses her closed eyes before they lock again and a look of permission is asked...and given...she slides across his skin, pulling him in to be tasted against her lips, hungry fingers drag down his back...the pain intensifies the passion as he drops down and dives into her midriff, tender kisses gorge on her belly button, passionate and all-encompassing she whimpers.

Through the touch, her back arching under his mouth, fingers running through his hair and still he continues, his hands sliding under her back and gripping her waist pulling her closer...as close as he can entangling becoming one, breathes chase heartbeats and echo off each other's exhale...and they stop...suddenly.

Red flame burns in their eyes, the pounding of chests demand justice, the justice of the broken ones piecing themselves together if only for one perfect night connected, their edges fit perfectly creating the most beautiful bliss pressed against time, she burns entirely against his embers, the smoke of their sex visible against a harsh horizon and the picture they create framed for an eternity splatters across each other, their own beautiful masterpiece stained by bodies and mouths and inked by words and poetry. The cruel ocean cannot fully separate these artists, cannot dilute or drown out how they feel about each other as they will forever collide on waves in souls and ink pressing boundaries and currents through each other's need...yet...

...their fantasies remaining fantasies, a dream of what could be but can never transpire...the torment felt, the torment shared, the broken and the broken lived on forever mixed in ink and dreams and a sliver of hope.

Only in my dreams

Encased within these four walls of loss,
the spotlight of the moon raptures through,
blinking in anticipation the stars watch
and my thoughts hitchhike a ride to you.

My rhapsody slows conquered by sleep,
invading my body now limp and free,
a deaf tone enters my mind's eye
for only in my dreams are you inside me.

Our burning displacement sends us hurtling towards one another,
erupting all around us this thunderstorm welcomes our sex,
the pounding rain soaks through sizzling skin boiling from our heat
as we carve out the veins of ink caressed by fingers eager to explore,
every hole is ventured sparking reactions of passion and wonder,
natures bedroom resides in our minds both special and unique.

Strangers eyes awaken to the show we suddenly writhe about in,
the voyeurs we welcome dance with their self-pleasure,
this motive needed to become stars inside a glorious performance,
fuck me this and fuck me that, unlimited positions...unlimited come,
like dolls ravaging away their porcelain shell revealing a savage flesh,
paid in green, sticking to the script, an unreal compliance.

Amongst pots and pans we sit entwined and bathed in refrigerator light,
splashed at naked feet are sweet ingredients demanding imagination's flame,
painting our bodies creamy white, smothered inside and out with a sugar rush,
the swirls of colour tasted and shared melting over curves of passion,
a canvas stretched by edible toys of size and bend that satisfies our hunger,
their innocence crooked and lost as we wallow in this gleaming mush.

Leather serenades the air sending a rush of nightmare filth into open arms,
its voice carrying an anticipation of hell bound pleasure torn and shared,
collapsing our senses with a snap of strained whips clawing at moist curves,
nothing to do but surrender to the chains as puppets to their masters,
the twist and turn of vessels breach limits into a forbidden lust of silence,

that place pain and pleasure share the absolute connection of wanton nerves.

Hypnotised within an illumination of fantastical games we play and create,
the endless costumes provide desolation of who we are and who we want to be,
monologues produce roles reversed, lines left behind and limits ripped apart,
shredding boundaries into jigsaw pieces re-used to build this citadel of taboo
and inheriting characters that allow us to sway our inhibitions and have some fun,
tearing and ripping cloth the unravelling outward bare merely the start.

Morpheus awakens exhausted you land entwined amongst duvet and pillow of mine,
we tumble in-between soaking sheets, the chorus of our moans deep and heavy,
I gorge on your lips, devour your pussy and willingly melt into your absorbing body,
honey overspills from my mouth, your wetness ready to be given and fucked,
slithering down my being you take me in and rise, your burning stare cages my soul,
grinding with intent and purpose soaring to a climax of a unified decree...and then...

...suddenly within these four walls of loss,
the searchlight of the sun raptures through,
blinking in disappointment the stars weep
and my wishes hitchhike a ride to you.

My heartbeat slows tricked by sleep,
invading my body now stiff and free,
a screaming pain enters my mind's eye
it seems only in my dreams are you inside me.

Paint a nice little picture that shows love

Can you?
No really, can you?

Write a sonnet that describes the feeling of love

Can you?
No really, can you?

Expunge out the words of poetry with the passion of love

Can you?
No really, can you?

Prove to me that there is such a thing called love

Can you?
No really, can you?

and from under this table I see...nothing.

I feel no love. I feel no respect. I feel no warmth. I feel...nothing.

I take a sip of my coffee that sits on the floor on a coaster and it is freezing cold. How long have I been here under this table?

There is nothing but silence...even from my own mind, it rests.

Where are the other voices? Where are the other screams? Where are the other people?

I crawl out from under this table and crawl back under then I crawl back out from under this table and crawl back under...and then I crawl back out from under this table. The wood has rotten, the nails holding it together rusted away and the surface is covered with mould.

I stand up...painfully.

My bones crack, my muscles cramp up and my head swims and spins...how long have I been there under that table?

I have discovered, travelled, mingled, hurt, been hurt, destroyed and created everything from under that table and now I am free...

...hell awaits. The table was the only thing protecting me from its grip...its madness...its revenge. For he awaits as well...goodbye.

finally, comfort runs dragged across bare arms in
lines of red and scratchy scratch

and darkness is the colour of death that swirls
around sticking to white teeth

a failed attempt to sew shut the voices using worn
out stitching and bent needles

finding myself locked in coffin of slinky
coldness dripping with a brilliant hatred of me

my arms tired from pushing the ones to the edge
of ceramic forgiveness

all the while protecting and comforting the
father inside of the son

this fighting an odyssey of celluloid reverse
promises grinning with lies

guiding my carcass over trenches of the last
final scar and fresh blood

and what's left but an echo of who I was shivering
under a table of wood

a splintered performance with a nod to the
crowd and a pitiful applause.

(dedicated to) The Last Of Us

Mountains of absence,
jagged like collar bone skin,
parchment lips kissed, explored and pulled through fingers,
white teeth...visceral purr.

Echoes from valleys red with ache,
blooming beneath fingertips that rush rivers from eyes and mouths,
hunger...desperation takes over...a blind stabbing,
bodies encased in candlelight,
warping into each other they sway and drown,
lungs fill with words – blacken with ink,
the air falls over heaving breasts splitting apart the slightest touch
and allowing interstellar pupils to consume this doomed traveller,
driven by visceral need and blinded eyes – we touch
between spills of open mouths and closed eyes,
breathing within the lungs that drown us,
chain smoking hearts only to feel the little deaths each time we inhale,
we grow black with time and our red ache spirals against each slipped word.

For all of this earth we fade apart,
our bodies surrounded by a liquid light,
witness to the fragment of our lust.

Yet darkness gives way to sun streak hair,
golden curls entwine around an exposed throat,
and lay waste across a naked chest,
the scent of starlight calling out to a battered heart,
the need for desire calling out to a broken mind,
"please my dear, capture me in this night and make me feel..."

Anything but lost within your fractured eyes,
those embers will ignite my skin and set a wildfire through my skin.
Never to be extinguished by stolen breaths and fingertips,
they will only grow wild on my lips scorching a mouth I
so desperately missed.

Yet this collision of taste and words
give tongues that spiral an eternal poetry,
we thrash against our sin, explore our haunting,
begin to carve out tattoo promises...inside and out.

We synch and I watch you rise on me,
crucified at your mercy, nailed to this bed,
afraid of your beauty, enlightened by your sex,
in awe of tears crashing over my broken body.

Bodies rise and fall, heartbeats against barren walls,
limbs entangle and eyes become salvation.
Allowing us to drink from lips and becoming one another's salvation.

Holy arches tremble and sanctuaries crumble beneath our breaths,
you are my retribution and I am your shame.
(We are to each other as much a saviour as a destroyer) as
poetry flogs our bodies and explores the taboo,
nothing but a pile of broken thresholds will remain,
we transcend pleasure and feast on our erotica,
tour the bodies we each give over to the other.

Lessons and marks stain lips,
poetry written across the skin as braille,
only touch deciphering our longing.

We collide as souls,
emerging as one heartbeat that holds the walls and secrets of intimacy...
...but these walls begin to crumble.

They reveal prison bars of ice that tear us apart,
this rib cage cold and claustrophobic silences the voice of my heart,
plunges it into dead space; a darkness so black I am forever blinded.

And so, lost and alone, I sway,
a criminal to my own mind,
a prisoner to my own hatred,
a spectre to my own haunting,
nothing left but memories of candles and incense.

Memories of candle and incense

what is this light?
beyond these four walls
there are memories of candle and incense.

I thought I heard a voice calling me,
I thought I heard a heart beating…
…that was my own voice ending
and my own heart breaking.

words spill out from freshly sliced wrists,
the blood evaporating into dust and cake.

wooden bones splinter and fall,
creativity caves in and becomes rotten, lost, burnt.

broken loses sight of broken,
those who once loved you are pushed away
detached and now a part of yesterday…
…they soon forget;
but then again, so do I.

I have forgotten happiness.
I have forgotten joy.
I have forgotten all that was.

but the enticing flame,
the smoke trail snaking,
a hint of heat,
a whiff of fragrance…

…nothing more than the flame of death's heart
and the stench of rotten bones,
he calls to me, chants my name, draws me closer
and closer
and closer…

chant

fucking
desire
hate
divinity
chant my name and spit

loneliness
chaos
blank
suffocate
chant my name and laugh

bury
hurt
sunset
slice
chant my name and forget

crack
scab
bleed
smile
chant my name and loathe

search
fly
flood
dream
chant my name and wail

haunt
obsess
mutilate
monologue
chant my name and accept

question
debate
insomnia
ink
chant my name and climb

gone
joke
suicide
end
chant my name and regret

Excuse me regret…

…any chance you can just fuck off?

Your timing is impeccable,
your words are too late,
a righteousness so insufferable
it carries no weight.

(Don't speak to me about consequences,
don't lecture me on what is right,
don't shake your head at my justification,
don't wiggle your finger in my face,
don't belittle the decision I made,
don't…don't…don't…)

It pumps ice through your skin,
chokes you with your own heart,
sends your mind into a spin,
turns self-harm into an art…

…regret…

Self-harm

I looked in the mirror staring at my reflection,
no emotion as the blade scores across my skin,
the world behind me laughs ignorance in bliss,
oblivious to this pleasure and pain within.

Weeping in disgust my body reacts with sorrow,
reeling as the blood trickles down red run,
screaming I find I don't know how to stop,
memoirs of suffering exposed to the glass sun.

Pieces of my mind vanish without a trace,
scars upon scars are left to redefine,
reminders of the person I have now become,
mommy's little boy long gone left to dine.

And so…

…dead eyes search for the tick tock of life,
finding nothing but a broken face,
exposure to a life led and suffered,
almost done now, not much left to erase.

Erase

Branches crawl across the mirror shattering its sandpaper reflection
and off to the races we go,
the horizon splits in half with a comedy of sadness soaked in piss
and off to the races we go,
quietly turning all the right heads for all the wrong reasons
and off to the races we go,
earning whispers that demand our existence becoming a simple erase
and off to the races we go,
even the wolves hiding in the walls come out to stare
and off to the races we go,
a dark paradise awaits those of us who pay with suicide currency
and off to the races we go,
time is buried in its own cemetery littered with poetry grave stones,
and off to the races we go,
hiding coffee stained coffin of grey clouds and thunderstorms
and off to the races we go...

...lets place a bet on the lucky ones brave enough to empty their wrists
for off to the races we go.

we go

hand in hand, my depression and I...we go,
much more than just my depression;
my despair,
my hatred,
my self-loathing,
my worthlessness,
my fucking mind,

though my eyes can now see in the dark,
the land we travel is barren,
howling winds whip in every direction,
batters around from every side...

...and the sky is lit by a black moon,

we walk over skeletons,
the bones cutting deep into my bare feet,
we walk over skulls,
the teeth biting down onto bare toes,
we walk over death,
the scythe slicing across bare wrists,

but on and on we go,
no end in sight,
no messiah to call us,
no oath to swear against,
no hope to guide us,
no words of comfort,
no love to help us...

...and then comes the rain...

The Suffer of Rain

Tiny pin pricks gently fall like feathers whispering in the snow,
grazing over bare skin as if teasing my senses with light.
Striking the ground tentatively and with an embarrassed hush,
they disappear in a fragmented star dust eruption of reaching digits.

Now with a little bit more meaning a waving blanket begins,
tucking over me in a harvest beyond the horizon.
A fine consistent wetness begins to seep into my being,
darken the ground I walk onwards to what I do not know.

Then comes the torrent undeterred or concerned with light,
a battering of ink marking my soul with determined words.
Crawling around and into every fibre of my corpse,
bouncing against anything it strikes as if re-joining the clouds.

And finally the suffer of rain becomes alive forced downwards,
slicing away my softened up flesh and muscle.
I feel my body fade away cut to pieces and butchered,
washed away amongst the rest of the sewage down hells drain.

Hell

...a cow was defecating the half-digested remains of butchers, their faces contorted, melted, their guts and acid eaten brains spilling out all over the floor. It turned to look at me as its tail swished from side to side brushing one of the faces playfully. The butchers moans and pleads went unnoticed as the cow turned its body round and began to eat the same butchers it had just shat out...their gurgling screams drowned out by the munching jaw of the cow.

I heard the unmistakable chatter of teeth and turned to see a man held down on his back by hands protruding from the ground. Gathered around him were demons in various stages of decomposition ripping him apart piece by piece. One of his legs had been torn off, his right arm had slices of flesh carved out, both eyes were in the process of being gouged away, a hand played about in his exposed cranium and his chest cavity was splayed open as one of the demons held aloft a lung in victory.

Moans of sick pleasure emanated from a far wall and I had to squint in order to focus on where they were coming from. A mass of naked people joined together by their own insides squirmed and writhed as one, their blood and muscle the paste that kept them together and the exposed nerves sending waves of erotic pain through their foul bodies; spit and cum a constant addition to their passion.

I felt a hand on my shoulder and spun round. A topless man stood staring at me. Scored across his torso were dotted lines sectioning off various parts of his body. His eyes were cue ball white and his skin, a cigarette stain of yellow. In his left hand he held a serving plate garnished with lush green leaves and salad bits. Suddenly, with his right hand, he pulled the skin off his whole left side, careful to stay within the dotted lines with each tear. Slamming these bits onto the serving plate, he offered them to me like a waiter would offer finger food.

I pulled free from his grip and fell backwards dragging myself away until I came to a wall banging my back against it with a stop. There was a sound of crawling and wriggling and I turned to the right. Propped up against the wall was half a man's body; no legs and no waist. His mouth and eyes were clamped open beyond breaking point and his arms were wrapped in barbed wire. A sea of maggots spilled out from his stomach, their bloated appearance suggested they had feasted on the missing legs and waist. His eyes looked at me and then downwards. I followed his gaze and came across his grey and shrivelled genitalia completely untouched by the maggots.

I screamed in silence and crawled away clambering to my feet and running at full pelt towards what looked like a door. I smashed through and landed on my face feeling the burn as it scraped across the rubble filled floor. Then I felt the heat and saw a vast landscape fall before me. Mountains with carved out faces bled larva from their eyes and mouths, skeletons flew across black skies that lit up with lightning made of fire and the wind was alive with a suffering littered with torture and desires. In the distance, a huge tower made of metal, pipes, gothic spires and cogs loomed into view. A centre piece sprouted arms of bridges that disappeared in all directions...indeed, one of which I had found myself on.

"That." said death suddenly appearing from behind me, "is where we are going." "What is that place?" I whispered. "That...is suicide...now get up and follow me." I stood up and we began to walk across the bridge. As we walked, I noticed there was a huge collection of people on the other bridges walking in the same direction; to the heart of this tower. I stopped. "Why are we the only ones on this bridge but the others are crammed full of people?" I asked death. "We are not the only ones on this bridge." he snarled walking on past me. I looked behind us...nothing. I looked ahead of us...nothing. I looked all around us in every direction...nothing. I was about to question his answer but thought the better of it and ran to catch up with him. A huge arch loomed into view and from it I could hear a chorus of wails and screams. As we passed through, the terrible sound was akin to the roar and rush of a great waterfall; overpowering the senses with noise and tangible thickness.

A business man sat slumped laughing against a wall, several pieces of his head blown off by the still smoking gun he held tight in his hand. A naked red haired girl wandered past me mumbling numbers. I watched as she staggered on, her body covered in self-inflicted slices from the rusty knife now buried into her stomach as she spilled free her own intestines. An old fat man in a blood stained vest eyed me up. He was trying to say something so I got in low but realised his throat was cut from ear to ear and jumped back in shock. As I stood, something sharp scraped across the top of my skull causing me to duck and look upwards. Hundreds, maybe thousands, of rotting and rotten bodies hung from the rafters. The nooses around their necks swayed them from side to side in a queasy unison.

"Welcome to the gallery!" death shouted pulling my attention away from above me. "How is this a gallery?!" I shouted back through quivering jaws as the full extent of this tower began to hit me. It was enormous and full of people re-living their suicides over and over; my god, I thought, these poor bastards are trapped...locked in this endless act. Even the bodies swinging above me clawed at their ropes, their eyes in a constant rattle and their tongues lolling out from their mouths. I felt something cold and hard in my right hand and looked down...it was a knife. Without even registering my actions, I sliced my left wrist severing the veins and releasing blood all over the floor.

There was an increase of that terrible sound within the halls that echoed throughout the tower causing it to ripple with energy and expand in size right before my eyes; I was adding credence and strength to this gallery of suicide. I dropped the knife and clasped my right hand over my wrist in an attempt to stop the bleeding squeezing as hard as I could but the blood seeped through my fingers and rushed out. The naked red haired girl bent down and picked up the knife I had dropped. She studied it intently, smiled at me and then continued to slice away at her body, the old rusty one now imbedded deep into her stomach and completely useless to her. It was then that I threw up...all over the old fat man. He didn't blink. He didn't shut his mouth. He didn't move. "Oh my god...I'm so sorry!" I stammered wiping my mouth and backing away as the chunks of my last meal dribbled over his eye balls, down his lips and into the open wound on his neck causing him to cough and choke.

I turned my back to him, ran over to a wall and threw up again sinking to my knees and slamming my hands flat out into the puddle of my own sick, blood and tears. "Do you want to spend eternity here reliving and re-enacting your suicide?" death whispered in my ear. I turned just in time to see a mess of bones crash onto the floor and shatter in every direction; there was complete silence throughout the tower. Looking up, I could see the skull the bones belonged to still hung from the noose, its jaw open wide when a pitiful cry begun to emanate from it. Death hauled me up, grabbed my bleeding wrist and healing the wound instantly. He then stood behind me and wrapped his arms tight around my body...I struggled to break free but he held me fast. "Trust me, you need to see this!"

Everyone else was perfectly still and looking down at the mound of bones or up at the hanging skull, its crying now that of a new born baby. Suddenly, there was movement. I watched as the bones dragged themselves back to each other, every single shard and piece re-joining with a sickening crack and snapping noise. It stood up, a complete skeleton once again, and began to shake. From the ground snaked upwards red thin wires. They pushed in between the toe bones and wrapped themselves within the entire skeleton mapping out throughout and creaking loudly as they did. A sound like that of a jet engine came from beyond the tower...and from all directions. A blur of colour and mass shot towards the skeleton and merged within it with the noise of a soaking wet mop being slapped on a stone floor. I stared in disbelief as organs settled...veins sprouting from them and shooting through the skeleton.

The skulls cries were now the screams of a young child as from the walls of the tower itself emerged slabs of muscle and flesh. The skeleton ambled over to each of the walls that housed said muscle and flesh and stood as they jumped onto it and slid into position with a slap. Once complete, the headless figure snapped its bloody fingers and skin floated from the sky and draped itself over the flesh, a breezy whoosh drifting through the air as it did. Now complete, I watched as it walked directly underneath the skull, whose cries were now screams, and launched upwards connecting with it with the sound of a shotgun going off. From the neck, the skull began to form...nerves, organs, muscle and skin all coming from the body until finally the last thing to sprout was the hair; beautiful long blonde hair that danced gracefully as it settled.

Her eyes shot open and her screams stopped. I realised that hanging above me was a teenage girl, no more than 15 years old I guessed. She looked all around her and lifted her hands to her neck. The noose gave a sudden jerk and tightened causing her eyes to roll backwards, her legs to kick out wildly and a muffled whimper to escape from her mouth...but it was drowned out by the returning noise inside the tower as every other soul returned to their own suicide. I started towards the girl but death grabbed me. I thrashed about violently against deaths grip but he was too strong and he dragged me out as I reached at the girl shouting at anyone and everyone to help her, tears bucketing down my face and encased in anger and hate but completely powerless to help her.

When we reached the outside of the tower, death threw me to the ground and I lay there weeping for a few moments until I became very aware that the bridge we had crossed was indeed full of people heading into the tower...just like death had said. I stood up slowly "Where did all these people come from?" I asked. "They were always here...you just weren't able to see them because part of you didn't believe." he grabbed my arm, "now you believe." he berated and led me away from the tower.

"So what happens now?" I said not really wanting to know the answer, "Why didn't you leave me back there...isn't that where I belong?" We stopped. Death turned, grabbed me, lifted me up and threw me off the bridge. I fell hard and fast. From within the darkness, words surrounded me. 'Caged, reduced to mindless...restricted. My life swamped with the mundane. A dead home, graveyard of innocence, feel for hell, both butcher and pig. Choirs grinning, that make love, numb...complete emptiness. An eternity or a fleeting glimpse, the beautiful, the continuation of nothing...hurt. Bullshit job to go to, not a chance, their insides out, suicide is the way...the end.' They strike me, pass through me and hurt me. I feel them inside me, burrowing into my chest and scratching at my skin. My heart is thrashing...I need to slow it down; I need to release it from its rib cage. Then I hear a voice. The voice of my father. "I hope this happens to you!" his tone grates like metal down a chalk board and I all of a sudden hit the ground with a dull thud.

"Death is like an open book, you just can't help but look, for on it in big red letters it reads, 'The End'...after all, that's all it means."

The Open Book

My spine has been broken,
pages of my story ripped apart,
words inside dead and stolen,
ink now bleeds from my heart.

Scattered about at my feet
commas and full stops die,
turned to ash in this heat,
not much left but a decry.

The open book sliced in two,
scissor writing pouring out,
letters begin to fade and undo,
losing what it was all about.

A wind disperses what is left,
forever gone in the night,
this all amounts to a simple theft,
and the end to an unwinnable fight.

Fight/Flight

Stop, start, stutter and breathe,
the wave length vibrates from left to right…right to left
and a heartbeat punches through the silence.

Veins bounce off the walls,
blood flows with tin like noise,
shake and shudder a mind unto death,
clap away with muscle and bone,
eerie lungs inhale…exhale…inhale…exhale
inhale liquid light and exhale butterfly words.

Twinkle twinkle cheetah thoughts,
dance to the monologue beat,
play ball with my brain…bound it off out four walls,
let me see a horizon of synth and oceans,
its bite floods my sight with amber and blue
sending me on a fear and loathing.

Pierce my hearing,
needles inside my head,
pluck tears from my cheeks,
collect them in urns,
bury them in the sky
and sail a vintage wind.

Soaring into the up,
battling into the down,
thick rhythms give credence to this flower,
petals like wings,
a stem like an engine,
growing within space…time havoc.

Strains and hardness shriek into my bones,
snapping and rearranging with melancholy,
infecting my dreams with coffee rain,
severing my feelings from my nerves,
spewing forth rainbows and branches…

Rainbows and Branches

I had a mother
I had a father
I had a mind
I had a love
now all I have are rainbows and branches

My rainbows arch in black
My branches hold no life

there was no life…

…in fear
…in hopelessness
…in despair
…in depression
…in hatred
…in self-harm
…in darkness
…in sorrow
…in principle
…in rot
…in ice
…in chaos
…in blades
…in division
…in soil
…in space
…in havoc
…in gods
…in demons
…in heaven
…in hell
…in divinity
…in love
…in heat
…in genesis
…in running
…in anyone
…in everyone

…in side

inside the mind of the dead

My eyes see what you cannot,
tainted,
portraying the hate inside,
outside,
my ears hear what you cannot,
unreal,
portraying the lies within,
falsely,
my touch feels what you cannot,
cold,
portraying the well-deserved,
loneliness,
my heart beats what you cannot,
heavy,
portraying the painful burden,
judgment,
my mind thinks what you cannot,
loathing,
portraying the ultimate madness,
completely,
my soul cries what you cannot,
caged,
portraying the lost boy,
forever...

...and my death is what you cannot,
understand,
portraying the depths I have fallen,
too far.

Fallen

Fallen too far I can't get up

Damaged too much I can't repair

Lost too many times I can't find my way...home?
Where was my home?
Where is my home?
Have I ever even had a home?

Hurt too deeply I can't heal

Battled too hard I can't defend

Despair too many times I can't find any...hope?
Where was my hope?
Where is my hope?
Have I ever had a hope?

Or has it all just been a fucking joke?

I started a joke

I started a joke
not realising I was the punchline,
a bad delivery
to a hungry crowd.

I started a joke
not understanding the full meaning,
a lost performance
to a silent theatre.

I started a joke
not seeing the funny side,
a lost comedy
to a stranded comic.

I started a joke
not wanting it to be over,
a final sketch
to a curtain call.

Yet when I started a joke
not me who even started it,
a supposed father figure
to a broken son.

broken son

broken...not even aware

broken...by something said so long ago

broken..."I hope this happens to you"

from father to son these words broke me,
from father to son these words infected me,
from father to son these words defined me,

and from father to son, these words are me.

me (the last of us)

And it's only the last of us that understand,
the lucky few that are forced to lose,
damnation from the womb,
cursed to the grave...we burn.

I never escaped those words,
never surfaced from under the table,
instead I lived within countless reflections
and died at the hands of countless scars.

The loop of insomnia and depression claws,
for eternity it wraps itself around my throat
whispering sweet every things into my eyes,
diluting my vision with cemetery darkness.

Lost, my mind crumbles away
and my heart grows cold,
so glad for the madness inside,
so glad for the flowers outside...

...me, I, us,
the son becomes the father's punishment,
the father becomes the son's innocence
and the world keeps on turning.

thank you

Once again, my heart and my thanks go to Michelle; beyond friendship, beyond love.xxx

To my Sister Joanne and my Uncle Geoff, and of course, to my cat Leia.xxx

To real friends, Steven Gibson, Chris Ratcliffe, Andrew Boyer, Steven Wills, and Derek Nuttall.

Social media friends...Sarah Giercksky, Emma Louise Hayes, Ash Watson, Elizabeth Faith K, Loreto Aguilar Castillo and Jennifer Jury, let's keep spreading the word, let's keep supporting each other's art.

Once again to my neighbours children Mac, Kennedy, Logan and Kara who kept me full of wonder (a wonder now sadly gone).x

To Emma, thank you for understanding, thank you for listening, thank you for helping.x

Huge thanks to Mark Cassell for the back cover insert design and inspiration for the final cover design

www.MarkCassell.co.uk   www.theshadowfabric.co.uk

Huge thanks to YouCaxton for an enormous amount of support and patience, especially Emma.

And to Heather Ranson, a fellow writer, a fellow artist, a fellow survivor...thank you.x

And of course to you, the reader.

Twitter - @absinthe666

Instagram – broken_finds_broken

And finally, to the artists, musicians, film makers and writers. Too many too mention but specific inspiration goes to the words of Chris Morris, the sounds (and album covers) of Cannibal Corpse and Cattle Decapitation, and the genius of Devin Townsend.

www.ingramcontent.com/pod-product-compliance
Lightning Source LLC
Chambersburg PA
CBHW071514040426
42444CB00008B/1636
9781911175698